Neither Stalin nor Hitler

JUKKA TARKKA

Neither Stalin nor Hitler

Finland during
the Second World War

HELSINKI
OTAVA PUBLISHING COMPANY

Published by arrangement with
Otava Publishing Company
Translation by David Mitchell
Printed in Finland by Otava
Printing Works Keuruu, 1991

ISBN 951-1-11824-2

Contents

Foreword by Max Jakobson   7

FINLAND SURPRISES   9
    The War Breaks Out   9
    The Wonder of the Winter War   12
    From Crusading to Security Policy   15
    Where Did the Spirit for the Winter War
    Come From?   17
    The January Betrothal   19
    Would Western Assistance Have Helped?   21
    Truce   22

FINLAND ADAPTS   26
    The Redivision of Europe   26
    Stalin's Summer   27
    A Transit Agreement   30
    Were There Any Alternatives to Germany?   32
    A Change of Guards   34

HITLER ATTACKS   36
    Who Knew and When?   36
    Where Was the Morality?   37
    When Could Finland Still Have Changed
    Course?   38
    SS Battalion   39
    Driftwood or Not?   42
    What Did Finland Want?   44

FINLAND JOINS IN   47
    Who Shot First?   47
    "Scabbard" Order of the Day   48
    A Separate War   50
    The Price of the Offensive   52
    Tanner's Line   54
    An Agreement to Please Hitler   55
    Ultimately on the Wrong Side   56

THE LULL IN THE WAR   59
    Mannerheim and Hitler   59
    Diplomatic Front   60

The Occupation of East Karelia 62
Finland's Refugee Policy 64
Censored Finland 65
Finland Begins to Falter 67

FINLAND DECIDES 69
Stalingrad and Leningrad 69
Peace Becomes Target of War 70
Attempts by the United States 72
The Race between the Government
and the Peace Opposition 75
Stalin Dictates 76

TOWARDS A SOLUTION 79
At the Crossroads 79
Paasikivi Tries 80
Psychological Bombing 82
Finland Still Waits 83
Hitler Threatens 86

ON THE BRINK OF THE ABYSS 88
The Miracle of the Karelian Isthmus 88
Political Chaos 90
The Road to Peace 92
The Guns Stop Speaking 93

THE BEGINNING OF A NEW ROAD 96
The Truce 96
The War in Lapland 98
The Control Commission 100
The Government Takes a Grip 102
The Stronghold of Peace and Democracy 104
The Price of War 107
Reparations 108
The Refugee Question 109
The Balance Sheet of War 110

Foreword

by Max Jakobson

Finland is relatively little known outside the country, even in Scandinavia. Media coverage of Finnish events is sporadic and fragmentary. This often upsets Finns. But they should be happy: No country that manages to stay out of trouble has much news value nowadays.

The last time Finland was at the center of world interest was more than fifty years ago, in the winter of 1939–40, when the country was invaded by the Red Army. The resistance of the Finns was greatly admired, byt they were left to their fate. Finland was written off as a free nation. But Finland survived, and we can now say: more than survived. Finland today is not only free but also prosperous, part of the European Free Trade Area, with a living standard as high as that of the rest of the Scandinavian community, a country living at peace with its powerful neighbour. The history of Finland, which used to be described as a series of narrow escapes from catastrophe, has turned into a success story.

There are in my view three main reasons for this favourable turn in the destiny of the Finnish people.

First, the Finns fought when they had to fight, and they defended themselves successfully. Apart from Great Britain and the Soviet Union, Finland was the only European country participating in the Second World War that was not occupied, neither by Germany nor by the Soviet Union. As a result Finland was able to maintain her independence and her political system intact throughout the war and after it. Her example shows once again that in a conflict between a great power with a wide range of interests and commitments and a small nation determined to defend itself, the balance of forces cannot be calculated by arithmetic alone.

Second, Finland stopped fighting in time and adjusted her policy to the realities of power prevailing in our part of the world. The lesson of the war was that neither Scandinavia nor the Western powers were able or willing to guarantee Finland's security against the Soviet Union. As an outpost of an anti-Soviet alliance Finland would risk in the event of a conflict to be overrun and abandoned, yet too small to be able to influence decisions on peace and war. Her security had to be based therefore on a policy of neutrality designed to assure the Soviet leaders that Finland would in no circumstances allow her territory to be used as a base or route of aggression against Russia. Finland's foreign policy has been conducted with prudence in order to ensure that no shadow of doubt would be cast upon this commitment.

The third and by no means the least important reason for Finland's success is the national cohesion and self-discipline of the Finnish people, as well as the vitality of her democratic institutions. The Finnish Parliament and electoral system have functioned essentially unchanged since 1906, and her present constitution has been in force since 1919. There are few countries in the world that can match this record of political continuity.

This book by the Finnish historian and columnist Jukka Tarkka is a concise, yet vivid analysis of Finland's policy during the Second World War. It is summed up in its title: In 1939, the Finns said no to Stalin; in 1944, they said no to Hitler. That is how Finland survived as an independent nation.

FINLAND SURPRISES

Finland became involved in the Winter and Continuation wars because the Second World War broke out in Europe. And that broke out for the most common of reasons; to correct the injustices in the previous Peace Treaty. The former water-colourist Adolf Hitler had developed a romantic state philosophy of blood, iron and race which had an obvious social foothold in Germany's spiritual soil. Hitler skillfully exploited the bitterness caused by the Peace Treaty of Versailles. An election victory lifted him to the position of Chancellor in January 1933 by almost legal means. Only afterwards did he stage a coup.

Germany resigned from the League of Nations announcing that the disgraceful Peace Treaty of Versailles no longer bound her. She began to arm herself embracing territory she considered German: Austria in March 1938, the German areas of Czechoslovakia in September 1938 and the rest of the country in March 1939. Next it was the turn of Poland.

The Soviet Union began to prepare for the worst. One month after Hitler had marched into Austria, Stalin's representative, Boris Yartsev, presented Finland with the question, that De-

The War Breaks Out

9

fence Minister Kliment Voroshilov had put to the Finnish Foreign Minister in February 1937: how could the Soviet Union obtain guarantees that Finland would not let her territory be used as a base for an attack on the Soviet Union. Yartsev asked for written guarantees proposing joint arrangements for the maritime defence of the Gulf of Finland. The Finns did not take him quite seriously and the negotiations were broken off in December 1938.

The Soviet Union tried again immediately after the occupation of Czechoslovakia by Hitler. Now she sent a more credible person than Yartsev who was formally only a Legation Secretary. Ambassador Boris Stein renewed Yartsev's proposals adding that the Soviet Union would like to lease some islands in the Gulf of Finland to be used for the defence of Leningrad. The Finns turned down these initiatives as well. Upon leaving Helsinki Stein said that the Soviet Union would not accept Finland's refusal but would return to the matter.

Stalin stated that European politics had entered a new phase where new men were required. Maxim Litvinov, who had made a reputation in the League of Nations, had to resign from his post as Foreign Minister in May 1939. He was replaced by a guaranteed Stalinist, Vyacheslav Molotov who began to break the Soviet Union's isolation in foreign policy by negotiating with Britain and France on anti-Hitler co-operation. The Soviet Union proposed an agreement to the West by which the Great Powers would guarantee the borders of small European states, but Britain and France announced that they did not want such guarantees. The negotiations stagnated.

Since Stalin was unable to conclude an agreement with the West over the event of an attack by Hitler he concluded a Treaty of Non-Aggression with him. This agreement of August 1939 was a sensational upheaval which in a moment turned the entire European political configurations on their head and thus also the environment in which Finland's security policy could function.

Throughout the 1930s Finnish foreign policy was based on a fear of the Soviet Union balanced by the threat of Germany on the Soviet Union. It was based on the assumption that the ideological balance of terror between Communism and National Socialism would prevent major upheavals. When Stalin concluded an agreement with his ideological arch-enemy no political compasses could be trusted.

There was suspicion in Helsinki that from Finland's viewpoint the Treaty would be even worse than what was told in public. The suspicion was well founded. The Treaty's secret appendix outlined Germany's and the Soviet Union's spheres of interest in Europe. Finland was included in that of the Soviet Union where Stalin had free reins.

To Hitler the Treaty of Non-Aggression was a sign that aggression could begin. Foreign Minister Joachim von Ribbentrop was hardly back in Berlin from the signing ceremonies when Hitler gave the order to his armed forces to attack Poland. But he experienced a big surprise: France and Britain which had meekly submitted to the Austrian and Czechoslovakian invasions now declared war on Germany following their treaty giving guarantees to Poland. Germany found herself in a war on two fronts. However, the West was not able to do much to interfere with Hitler's "blitzkrieg" in Poland.

Stalin scrupulously adhered to the Treaty of Non-Aggression that he had concluded with Hitler. The Soviet Union occupied her parts of Poland before Hitler's troops had reached Warsaw. In the course of the early autumn Stalin dictated his military political demands to Estonia, Latvia and Lithuania forcing them into an agreement of mutual assistance. This not only changed the security policy of the Baltic states but also their form of government within less than one year.

The Wonder of the Winter War It was the turn of Finland in October 1939. Negotiations in Moscow immediately revealed that the Soviet demands had been tightened because the situation in Europe had led to war. The peace-time proposals by Yartsev and Stein were no longer enough. Now Stalin demanded in addition an agreement of mutual assistance, a base on the Finnish mainland and that the border be pushed back in the Western part of the Karelian Isthmus in places by about 70 kilometres.

Finland did not agree to the treaty of mutual assistance, nor did she want to give bases and she did not bargain enough on the border question. She only agreed to smallish changes in the border at the bottom of the Gulf of Finland. When the negotiations broke off the dispute over the border concerned no more than 20 kilometres of territory. Finland still rejected the Soviet demands for a base on the Finnish coast. This led to the Winter War on 30th November 1939.

The Soviet Union commenced the war by a political offensive. She founded a peoples' government at Terijoki led by the veteran communist O.W. Kuusinen, the legendary leader of the reds who lost the 1918 bloody Civil War. In the final stage of the war he fled to the Soviet Union and became the secretary of Comintern, an international communist organization and the ideological ghost writer for Stalin. For independent Finland born out of the victory of the whites Kuusinen was a deeply traumatic figure even before the Winter War. A short-term period of government at Terijoki secured him a permanent place in the Finnish chamber of horrors for historical monsters; he became the living monument of treason.

The crude revolutionary propaganda of the Soviet Union made certain that nobody took Kuusinen's government seriously, least of all the Finns. During the first few days of the war the basis of Finnish government broadened and Risto Ryti became its Prime Minister. The Finns grouped to support this government in a desperate defensive battle.

The first wonder of the Winter War was political. The Finnish communists took up arms to oppose the Soviet Union and Kuusinen's government. A feeling of nationalism overcame international ideology although there was less than a generation since the bitter defeat of the reds. The workers that were defeated in the 1918 Civil War lost nearly 25 000 people, the winners arbitrarily executed about 7000 of them and 12 500 died of starvation in prison camps. The brothers and sons of the red martyrs who had fallen in vain on behalf of Soviet Finland rose in the Winter War to defend white Finland against the Soviet Union.

The second wonder of the Winter War was

military. Finland held out. A static trench warfare was fought on the Karelian Isthmus. In it the Finns first withdrew a few dozen kilometres and then dug into a main defensive position which held out till February. In the early phase of the war, the Finns had their worst difficulties in the area between Lake Ladoga and the Arctic Sea; the most critical battles were fought 500 kilometres north of Leningrad. There, going strictly by the book, great numbers of Soviet troops penetrated along all negotiable roads towards Finland's interior. Finns had little power and even that was dispersed. A surprise defence which broke all regulations had to be developed against an orthodox military attack. Desperate circumstances created a myth of encirclement.

In these decisive battles Finns were forced to develop their lack of power into a virtue which looked like military genius. Ill-equipped and weak in numbers, the Finnish units unscrupulously attacked heavy motorized enemy divisions jammed up in forest roads. The Finns proved that even a great military power which is stuck in place can become disordered and be destroyed with surprise attacks, harassment and attrition by small but fast troops.

The secret of the Finns' success was a bold initiative despite disadvantageous relative strength. Their firing power was not sufficient to cripple the enemy forces. So they had to use mobility. This unprejudiced and dangerously bold way of waging war was obviously influenced by the fact that Finnish officers were fairly young; the average age of generals was around 40 at the outbreak of the Winter War. Young men endured the mental and physical pressures of the desperate war and were able to conduct a more mobile war than a bureaucratized great military power.

The Winter War was decided politically in the first one-and-a-half months. After that the war went into a military phase which led to the supremacy of the stronger. But the war did not end in Finland's military collapse and was therefore resolved on the basis of the political result achieved in its first few weeks.

Since Finland warded off the Soviet demands in the autumn 1939 negotiations, Stalin ordered the Leningrad military district headquarters to prepare a military solution to the problem and it undertook it on 30th November 1939. Until the beginning of January 1940 the war was mainly a war of the Leningrad military district against Finland and its goal was political; to compel Finland to the concessions demanded by converting her into a socialist state.

From Crusading to Security Policy

After the Kremlin had realized that the solution would not come about on a local level it took the reins into its own hands. On 7th January 1940 it formed a North-Western Front which was under the Soviet Minister of Defence. He was given a military objective, the number of troops against Finland was nearly doubled, and the war was conducted in accordance with classical war strategy.

Finland still had her chances in a local war, but in a national war waged by a great power the situation was different. The Leningrad military district fought the Winter War for a couple of months with moderate success. The Soviet Union achieved the upper hand within a month.

From Finland's point of view, however, the most decisive change was Moscow's announcement at the end of January 1940 that it would consent to negotiate with the government in Helsinki. Kuusinen's term of government lasted only as long as the Leningrad military district led the war. It could afford to think of things other than national security politics. It fought an ideological war and as long as it was such it was a question of life or death for Finland. Various compromises can always be built from military and political factors but it is much harder to bend ideology the same way.

The Kremlin thought of Soviet politics from the point of view of great power interests. That Kuusinen was rejected indicated that a great power cannot afford to bind ideology with its security policy. The Soviet Union decided to accept that her North-Western neighbour would remain Capitalistic because converting her to Socialism had proved difficult. The Kremlin's political goals in respect to Finland could be achieved in many different ways. From its perspective it would have been excellent, had the Leningrad military district succeeded in elevating Kuusinen to the position of Prime Minister in the Helsinki government and converting Finland into a Socialist country. But the stubborn resistance of the Finns prevented that. The Kremlin used other means. It changed from an ideological crusade to ordinary security policy.

Obviously the Winter War played a very central part in the emergence of post-war Fenno-Soviet relations. Not only because it retained Finland's independence but also because it showed that the Soviet Union had only military interests as far as Finland was concerned.

In a desperate situation the Finns fought furiously. This showed the stubborn trust of the peasants in the power of justice. It was a completely different kettle of fish from the usual mode of thinking in international politics which calculated the equation of many unknown variables between the relations of resources available, the probable result and losses to be expected. Apparently the behaviour of the Finns made such a great impression on the world and the Soviet Union, because it was so exceptional and illogical.

The Finnish defence forces were dismally prepared in the material sense. The success of a defensive battle was based on the organization of Civil Guards, a voluntary organisation which was made up of the white army that had won the 1918 Civil War. Finland's extremely efficient system of mobilization was based on this organization. However, its real task was military training and the upholding of a patriotic spirit. It succeeded well in both tasks. Naturally you cannot wage a war with spirit alone but without it you will not succeed either even if weapons were available. After all, weapons can somehow be obtained even after the outbreak of war, but creating the right spirit may then be too late.

Finland had the spirit for the Winter War even before it actually broke out; thanks to the Soviet Union. Prompted by the threatening politics of Moscow voluntary fortification work was already carried out in summer 1939 along the most vulnerable parts of Finland's Eastern border. After the negotiations in Moscow began in the autumn Finland de facto mobilized herself although it was called extra training for recruits. During these preparation stages a red proletariat and the student son of a white family dug soil

Where Did the Spirit for the Winter War Come From?

together on the Karelian Isthmus and understood that the work and threat were common.

The unity during the Winter War was no surprise and did not break any historical lines. It was the result of societal developments during the period between the Civil War and the Winter War.

The losers of the Civil War were quickly pardoned. The former reds grouped themselves into a Social Democratic Party which adopted Nordic parliamentarism. Its leader, Väinö Tanner, became the Prime Minister of a minority government only a decade after the war. In this capacity he had to review the festive parade of the white Civil Guards in May 1927. In the period of the Great Depression in the early 1930s an extreme right-wing movement dominated Finnish domestic politics for a couple of years with aggressive speeches and violence. Even then the Social Democrats defended a Western democracy as they did in the Winter War. From 1937 onwards the winners and losers of the Civil War sat in the same government. General C. G. E. Mannerheim who had led the whites to victory in the Civil War recommended that Social Democrats join the Civil Guard.

Thus the spirit for the Winter War was not created so much by a sudden threat from outside but by the internal strength of the Finnish society. Had the wonder of the Winter War been a miracle, it would have been a passing phenomenon. Since it was a result of historical development it had many permanent features.

In a way it was the Communists who decided the outcome of the Winter War. They placed more importance on national values than on international ideology.

The claim that the Communists played a decisive role is not based on the idea that they would have had the strength to bring down Finland's form of government and that, after conscious deliberation they would have decided not to use this power. In autumn 1939 support for them and their organizational strength was very limited indeed. But the Soviet attack placed them mentally and politically into a position where the de facto significance of their decision was much larger than their political weight.

If the Communists had detached themselves from the national effort, it would not have come into being although the gap left in it by them would have been fairly small. The decision chosen by the Finnish Communists was of such significance because it was not born on the organizational level but through the genuine feeling of the people themselves. In its way, it was the victory of patriotic spirit over matter. Then, long after the war, it became apparent that the Communists chose a good role, even in a material sense.

The January Betrothal

The trade union movement and employers' organizations had sullenly gone their separate ways throughout the post Civil War period. They were interest organizations that did not negotiate with each other. The threshold for collaboration had remained so high because it was burdened with a two-fold ideology. The Socialist theory behind the trade union movement's political strength naturally stemmed from the idea that the conflict between work and capital cannot be reconciled.

This was the standard ideological threshold.

The attitudes of the employers were totally permeated by right-wing thinking which was still powerful long after the Civil War. They considered the trade union movement unpatriotic because its organizations were so strongly involved in the so-called rebellious activities of the reds. There was no talking to them.

Mannerheim's and Tanner's policy of rapprochement proceeded with caution and, in the 1930s, laid the groundwork for the change which was inevitably coming. The extra training for the recruits arranged in the autumn of 1939 finally changed the last vestiges of these attitudes. Personal contacts across class barriers efficiently moderated old ways of thinking.

The rigid structure of organizations gave way to new attitudes soon after. This would undoubtedly have happened without the Winter War but its extreme pressure gave momentum to them.

In January 1940 the Central Organisation of Finnish Trade Unions and the Finnish Employers' Confederation made a joint declaration recognizing each other as negotiation partners. However, this meant no collective agreement, in fact not really an agreement at all. It was only a declaration that negotiations and agreements, which were impossible earlier, could now take place.

The January betrothal is the starting point for modern incomes policy. It broke the ice in labour market policies. However, in the conditions prevailing in the Winter War it was mostly of general political significance and was linked more with the spiritual status of society than with incomes policy. Its message to the Finns themselves and the outside world was that of national unity.

It is said that in an emergency situation you grasp at straws. During the weeks of the Winter War, Britain and France produced ever grander plans for dispatching troops to Scandinavia. It appeared that they were helping Finland. Therefore Finns gave careful consideration to these offers. They seemed to give a real alternative, particularly as the other option was only submission to conditions dictated by the Soviet Union.

Basically they had very little to do with helping Finland. The Scandinavian operations planned by the Allies threatened Sweden in roughly the same way as did Moscow's proposed negotiations with Finland in autumn 1939. The point of departure for the policy pursued by Britain and France was not so much the Winter War as the mineral deposits in Sweden. They were also hankered after by Germany and the Soviet Union who at this stage were allies. Therefore the Western Powers would not have willingly given them to either; they wanted them themselves.

The longer the Winter War continued the more likely would the Soviet troops have reached the northern border between Finland and Sweden. The closer to the mineral deposits the Soviet Union was the more certain was it that Hitler would try to get there before Stalin. And the more obvious it became that Hitler attempted to improve his position in northern Sweden the more certain it was that the Western Powers would try to gain a foothold there before Germany.

All alternatives were equally bad from Sweden's viewpoint. It appeared that she could only determine who would occupy her territory and burn her towns. These multiple problems could be solved in one way only; by the speedy end to the Winter War. Peace between Finland and the

Would Western Assistance Have Helped?

21

Soviet Union could be of almost any kind, it would strip the Western Powers of the excuse for sending troops to Scandinavia and would prevent Sweden from becoming a battlefield between the Allies and Germany.

From Finland's point of view, seeking the assistance of the Allies was really grasping at straws. If the armies of the Western Powers had headed towards Karelia via the Atlantic and Scandinavia they would have afforded only a fractional force – 6 000 men – to the Finnish front and even they would have arrived far too late – towards the end of April 1940. However, the Allies' plans were of political advantage to Finland.

As long as the Allies' plan for Scandinavia was topical, the Soviet Union was forced to take it into consideration. It strengthened the position of those Kremlin leaders who preferred a negotiated agreement concerning the Finnish question more than a military solution. In the final analysis the Allies' planned military expedition to Scandinavia served Finland best as long as it was only talked about. Putting the plan into operation would have caused great political difficulties and produced very little military benefit.

Pulling out of the war was very difficult for Finland since the counterpart was a powerful great nation. How much more difficult it would have been if two great powers had sat around the peace negotiation table on Finland's side!

Truce

The Winter War ended with the Peace Treaty of Moscow signed on 13th March 1940. Finland lost more land areas than she had in the battlefield. The entire Karelian Isthmus had to be ceded to the Soviet Union, likewise the eastern parts of Kuusamo and Salla as well as the Kalastajasaarento peninsulas in Petsamo, plus the islands in the Gulf of Finland that Finland had refused to hand over in the negotiations of 1939. Additionally Finland had to lease out the country's southernmost peninsula, Hanko. The only concession achieved by Finland was that there was no longer talk of the agreement of mutual assistance demanded in the autumn 1939 negotiations.

Territorial concessions thoroughly upset Finland's economic and topographic structure. Material losses were astronomical when Finland's economy at that time is taken into consideration. Human losses were crushing – 22 000 dead and 43 000 wounded, and the spiritual burden left by the war was overwhelming. On the basis of all this it could be argued that Finland lost the Winter War.

It is true that the war ended in an unbearable situation at the fronts. Finland had not yet suffered a military defeat but had the fighting continued, the result would have been a downright catastrophe. However, politically the war was a victory.

Finland achieved her most important goal; she remained independent. The Winter War made the Soviet Union decisively change the basis of her policies towards Finland. She separated ideological goals from those of security policy and started to apply general security policy principles to Finland as well.

Finnish national unity manifesting itself in the Winter War obviously left a stronger imprint on the political souls of the Kremlin leaders than it did on the Finns themselves. The Finnish working class had very tangibly shown that it had other things to loose than its shackles, and these it defended.

The Soviet Union learnt a lot in the Winter War. Her army had to test its fighting skills in extremely harsh conditions. She did not do particularly well in this dress rehearsal. She began strengthening both her armament and military training.

Perhaps a greater political lesson was local but also political. The furious fighting by the Finns proved that even if their country could perhaps be conquered militarily, governing it would be extremely difficult.

The Peace Treaty of Moscow marked the beginning of a period which had a name even before it had really commenced. As the government was negotiating conditions for peace, Defence Minister Juho Niukkanen said that he considered the Treaty a Truce and Prime Minister Ryti announced that he agreed. The Great War was still going on in Europe and almost anything could happen, even miracles.

March 1940

■ Territory of Germany and its Allies

≡ Territory conquered by the Soviet Union

When the Winter War ended trench warfare continued in Western Europe, Germany and the Soviet Union had settled the division of Poland.

Following map on page 28.

FINLAND ADAPTS

The Redivision of Europe

On the Finnish horizon winter 1940 was a time of stormy events and drama. The rest of Europe still lived in an almost drowsy expectation of great events. It had plenty of time to admire how Finland fought for her life. For other Europeans the fierce drama of their war began in the spring when Finland had had time to take a breather. It changed the entire continent even more thoroughly than Hitler's and Stalin's agreement had done the previous summer.

Germany narrowly beat Britain and secured her grip on the North Atlantic. With a ruthless lightning strike she occupied Denmark and Norway on 9th April 1940. Germany put the mineral wealth of Sweden beyond the reach of the Allies. She controlled the entire length of Norway's sheltered coastline from where she could efficiently threaten Britain's fleet.

A month later Hitler shook the world even more profoundly. A German tank and air force attacked France across the fortified Maginot Line on 10 May 1940. Belgium and Holland surrendered within a couple of weeks and Britain was hardly able to withdraw her troops to the safety of home territory.

Now two great powers ruled Europe. Finland had no reason to expect anything good from either of them. They were allied and it seemed that they were respecting each other's interests and their mutual commitments more conscientiously than great powers had done for a long time.

In the early summer of 1940 the world certainly looked a gloomy place.

Stalin's Summer

The redrawing of Europe's political map in summer 1940 was not only Hitler's doing. At the same time that France was collapsing, Stalin began spreading his influence in the Baltic States with a heavy hand. By July Estonia, Latvia and Lithuania had become Soviet States.

The history of Fenno-Soviet relations for summer 1940 was a history of new demands and a diplomatic defence battle. The situation was distressing: the winner of the recent war was now demanding things that were clearly outside the scope of the Treaty. Each new demand alone was frightening to Finland and their overall effect felt worse than their sum.

The Soviet Union demanded the nickel mined in Petsamo near the Arctic Ocean. It was Finland's only remaining economic trump which the Soviet Union threatened to strip.

The Soviet Union demanded and was granted an overly large consulate in Maarianhamina in the Åland Islands. A demilitarized Åland threatened Finland's vital links with the West.

Transit traffic to the Hanko base meant that Soviet military trains continuously passed through the most important railway junctions in southern Finland.

27

July 1940

Territory of Germany and
its Allies

Territory conquered by
the Soviet Union

Hitler's surprise attacks first to the north and then to
the west decisively altered Europe's military geogra-
phy. The new situation emerging in summer 1940
forced the Soviet Union to tighten its grip; it took the
Baltic States under its control and presented Finland
with demands exceeding the regulations of the Peace
Treaty of Moscow.

Previous map on page 25.
Following map on page 43.

Moscow gave open support to the Fenno-Soviet Society of Peace and Friendship established by Finnish Communists. It seemed to be a clear political message dressed up as a threat because the Society's activities were mostly provocative.

In the eyes of the Finns, all this seemed like the beginning of the end. Yet the Soviet Union's treatment of Finland differed from that received by the Baltic States, which she took over without further ado. The experience of the Winter War could explain the difference but it also had a geographical explanation. Finland was further away from Leningrad, almost at its rear, whereas the Baltic States were along the route of attack on Leningrad.

Finns felt that the new Soviet demands and the fate of the Baltic States indicated Moscow's intention to finish off Finland as it had done to Estonia. There was political conformity because the motive behind Soviet action was the same both in Estonia and in Finland: the growth in Hitler's strength, in other words the Soviet Union felt more threatened than before. But the same motive does not automatically lead to similar action. The Soviet Union was content with less in Finland than in Estonia because Finland's location was different.

The Peace Treaty of Moscow fulfilled the security policy demands that the Soviet Union had in March. Europe's situation was totally different in summer. The Soviet Union in fact presented Finland with completely new demands outside the Peace Treaty of Moscow; but they did not stem from any changed goals she might have had in her policy. She had ended up in a situation where she no longer had a policy on

Finland. All she had was the policy of her own security. Everything she did in relation to Finland arose from this policy, not from Finland.

The development of the situation in Europe proves that the Soviet Union's new demands were part of a systematic security policy, although they were an abomination to the Finns. They felt that they had landed on the gallows; the thought of the logical grounds for hanging does not give much comfort to the one who feels the rope around his neck.

A Transit Agreement

Finland's political situation changed decisively in July 1940, unbeknown to the Finns at the time. Hitler's decision to attack the Soviet Union also meant that he needed collaboration with Finland. This began to manifest itself immediately.

The first sign was the visit to Helsinki by Dr. Ludwig Weissauer, a secret agent from the German Foreign Ministry, at the end of July. He attempted to find out the real willingness of the Finns to fight in the event of a Soviet attack. The question included a message, but this was hard to interpret at that point.

At the same time that the bombing of London was at its heaviest, a change took place in Finland's political position. Hermann Göring's emissary, Lieutenant Colonel Joseph Veltjens, flew to Finland in mid-August 1940 and with little ado sought to contact Marshall Mannerheim and Prime Minister Ryti. He got straight down to business. He promised that Germany would sell arms to Finland, if Finland allowed transportation of German troops via her territory to northern Norway. From the Finnish perspective the priority was on the sale of arms. Finland had attempted to buy arms for a long time so Veltjens' offer was a great relief. The question of transit was also very important in principle but perhaps not so extraordinary as it appears nowadays. It was not known then what the result would be.

During a war a lot of troops move on foreign soil, also through states which are not involved in the war. Sweden had just allowed German military transport on her railway. The Finns so badly needed German weapons and even a small gesture of political support from Berlin that permission to allow transit was almost self-evident. So self-evident that no Finnish politicians noticed that they had made such a decision, or at least did not admit doing so. They finally began to see a flicker of light at the end of the tunnel.

The agreement on Soviet troop transportation to the leased out naval base of Hanko was signed on 6th September 1940 and the agreement concerning German troops a week later. However, the first foreign troops to arrive on Finnish soil were German. They had been sailing towards Finland for a couple of days before their right to land was sanctioned.

When the first German ships docked in Vaasa on 22nd September 1940 the matter was still so secret that not all government ministers knew about it. The Vaasa police authorities asked the Minister of the Interior Ernst von Born for instructions as to what to do with the German troops that had docked early that morning. Woken up by the telephone call the Minister asked whether they were carrying passports.

Were There Any Alternatives to Germany?

The situation after the Winter War was desperate. There were only bad alternatives on offer and even they were merely theoretical. Those who have subsequently criticized the Continuation War easily think that seeking co-operation with Germany was predestined and self-evidently the only alternative. That was not the case. After the Winter War Finland's relations with Germany were worse than ever before. Sweden did not help much in the war but at least offered sympathy, Germany did not even offer that.

Finland reacted to her extreme political isolation in accordance with a Nordic model that had its roots in the interim between the World Wars. She felt out the possibilities of forming a defence union with Sweden, but the proposal met with no response. Only the hardest choice was left; to follow every regulation of the Peace Treaty of Moscow to the last letter and hope that that would suffice.

That road seemed to lead to destruction. From June onwards Moscow presented a series of demands that Finns felt were outside the scope of the Treaty. The transparently staged merging of the Baltic States with the Soviet Union seemed to indicate that the pessimists were right.

Not much ability at political analysis was needed to understand that Germany was the only alternative. But it seemed impossible to build hopes on that. Hitler remained Stalin's ally and scrupulously played his part; he remained aloof from the Sovietization of the Baltic States just as carefully as he had from the Winter War.

The first signs of awakening German interest in Finland in summer 1940 today seem self-evident. At the end of July, Hitler made a decision in principle to attack the Soviet Union. And only two weeks later Germany's representative was selling arms in Helsinki and agreeing on transit permission.

Naturally the Finns were able to interpret the arrival of Veltjens as a sharp change in German politics. But nobody could know how sharp and fateful. Therefore counting on Germany remained foolhardy. Only guesses could be made as to the background to Hitler's new mode of operations. It appeared to have changed so suddenly and completely that a new change of course seemed possible.

The Finns felt that the transit of German troops did not bind them to Germany. In fact it was only then that Finland began seriously to examine the possibilities of a defence union and even an alliance with Sweden. Finns felt that an alliance was an alternative worth taking seriously, above all for the reason that they wanted it so much more than collaboration with Germany. It ceased to be an alternative only when both Germany and the Soviet Union rejected it with determination in December 1940.

Finland committed herself to collaboration with Germany at the end of December 1940 because the other more enticing option had disappeared beyond the political horizon. But the main reason was that the future direction of development began to be visible between the lines of German speeches. Only at this stage did Germany begin to seem an enticing partner. But not because the leaders of Finnish foreign policy saw anything particularly desirable in Hitler's Germany but because recapturing Karelia seemed irresistible.

A Change of Guards

Finland had come a long way in 1940. She had experienced the days of agony and splendour in the Winter War, the nearly complete political isolation in spring and early summer and relief when collaboration with Germany finally began.

At the background to the politics that led to the Winter War was the Finnish conviction that justice would win and honesty would inherit the earth. It was only Mannerheim and the grand old man of the Conservative Party, J. K. Paasikivi, who preached the cold power politics of the Great Powers. Before Finland's independence Paasikivi had supported a flexible policy of appeasement towards Czarist Russia, during the First World War he leaned towards Germany and in the period between the World Wars he wanted Scandinavian co-operation to be the backbone of Finland's foreign policy. In the Winter War power was grasped by a trio of cold-thinking realists which included Paasikivi and Tanner as well as Prime Minister Risto Ryti. Ryti was a political wonder child in the early decades of independent Finland and a presidential candidate at the age of 35. He was a bookish intellectual and a strict-line economist. Under the pressure of war he developed an ability for Machiavellian sharp political analysis and cold rational decision making. The trio's security policy was conducted on the basis of the same cold reasoning, as that of the great powers. After all Finland had to adapt to their field of force.

The government's leading trio did keep President Kyösti Kallio up to date but he had no decisive influence over matters. The trio blasted their way to the Peace Treaty of Moscow although there was a deep-seated mistrust of the Soviet Union among both politicians and the people.

During the Truce, Ryti and Mannerheim continued the same cold line of rational politics that they had adopted under the pressures of the Winter War. In the field of international politics they played the same game as others. They consciously played the Soviet Union and Germany against one another as soon as an opportunity presented itself. They took the risks involved in playing for large stakes but there was no such option available with a small or even moderate risk.

The old foreign policy thinking that trusted in the power of justice disappeared completely when President Kyösti Kallio dramatically died at the Helsinki railway station while he was reviewing the guard of honour after he had resigned from office. In that year Finland's foreign policy changed from the era of peasant leaders and lawyers to the time of Machiavellian statesmen under which it continues to live.

HITLER ATTACKS

**Who Knew
and When?**

It is a clear exaggeration to claim that the Finns when deciding on transit permission in September 1940 knew that they were embarking on Hitler's crusade against the Soviet Union in June 1941. Likewise it is an exaggeration to claim that the Finns understood the matter only after the Germans explained it to them in detail in May-June 1941. They could deduce this or that from what was happening around them.

In all probability the decisive moment was 16th December 1940. It was then that Colonel General Franz Halder, the Chief of General Staff of the German army asked Major General Paavo Talvela, whom Mannerheim had sent to see him, how long the mobilization of the Finnish army to the south-eastern border would take. High-ranking commanders do not ask such questions out of idle curiosity. Talvela must have immediately understood that what was at stake was Germany's military preparation in the East. The first offensive operational plans were outlined at the General Headquarters in the week following Halder's and Talvela's discussion. Thoughts such as these had been carefully buried after the

Winter War. But now the soldiers understood that something new was in the making and they immediately began to think along lines that had not been possible for some time.

Halder received itemized answers to the questions he had presented to Talvela when Lieutenant General Erik Heinrichs, Chief of the Finnish General Staff, visited Germany at the end of January 1941. He had permission from the Finnish political leadership to reveal the country's operational preparedness and to outline the grouping of its main troops to the highest military leadership of a foreign power. Such powers are not granted unless the political leadership is fairly certain of the general line of development and unless it has decided to support that line.

Where Was the Morality?

In December 1940, or at the latest in January 1941, Finland embarked on a security policy that linked her fate with Germany. She chose this mainly because the Soviet Union seemed supremely threatening. Thus Finland bought security and paid a political and moral price for it. At least it seems like that nowadays when Hitler is not just any historical figure but a symbol of the moral degradation of mankind.

The value of the security policy decision must, however, be weighed against the consequences of such policies. The Finnish foreign policy leadership did not think of morality nor did it make a decision on ideological grounds. Security policy is always, and especially in times of major wars, above all the gospel of survival. Granting transit permission to German troops in August 1940 and entering into discussions on mobilization in

1940–1941 did bind Finland to Hitler. As such it was neither good nor bad. The question was whether it would improve Finland's political position from what it had been in summer 1940. Compared to this almost any change at all was a change for the better.

Even during the Truce, Paasikivi taught that Finland must adapt her security policy to the overall situation prevailing in Europe at any given moment. It meant that if the situation changed the policy had to be changed. If Germany was strong it was a matter of indifference whether the Chancellor, Kaiser or Hitler ruled in Berlin. This had to be taken into account in any event. If the Soviet Union seemed to be threatening Finland, help had to be sought wherever it was available, even if it was Germany. At least according to his memoirs, Paasikivi preached these two things to the leadership almost daily.

Ideologically Ryti leaned as little towards Hitler as the political leader of the post-war years, Paasikivi, leaned towards Stalin. On the basis of his major political deductions and under the weight of the overall situation, Ryti ended up co-operating with Hitler on security policy in the same way that Paasikivi did with Stalin after the war.

When Could Finland Still Have Changed Course?

During the Truce Finland took several decisions which can be considered the reason for getting into the war and the misfortunes that followed from it. These moments of fateful decision included at least the transit permission for the German troops in August 1940, the decision to reply to Halder's question in January 1941 and the decision to send a delegation of officers to Germany in May 1941.

Describing these decisions as decisive contains the wrong presumption, however, that some other choice in these situations would later have produced a different end result. Hitler would not have cancelled his attack on the Soviet Union even if Finland had denied transit in August, even if Heinrichs had not replied to Halder in January and even if Finnish officers had stayed at home in May.

An attitude of rejection towards Germany in these matters would have changed the way in which Finland got mixed up in Hitler's campaign. But no option available to Finns could have freed them from the nightmare that Hitler caused to the whole of Europe. In the course of progress that led to the Continuation War there was no such junction where Finns could have chosen war or peace. Hitler had made that choice on behalf of the whole continent.

SS Battalion

The permission for transit alone indicated that Germany's political interest in Finland had awakened. Finns attempted to strengthen it by all possible means; the desire was to make Germany a counterweight to the Soviet Union and her threatening attitude. Finland's struggle for independence had a legendary link with the Germany of the First World War. From 1915 onwards the anti-Russian resistance movement organized military training for Finnish men in Germany. This, about a 1 500-man strong core group formed the 27th Jaeger Battalion and most of them returned to Finland in February 1918.

39

The Jaegers did not make it home so soon as to be able to claim that theirs was the decisive role in turning the Civil War into a victory for the whites. But they became the backbone of the Finnish army and the celebrated heroes of the independence myth. Their patriotic sacrifices were more important to Finns than the fact that they had received their military training in Germany. Their links with Germany were, however, political capital that could be put to use during the Second World War.

In accordance with the Jaeger tradition the idea of sending a group of volunteers to Germany was expressed almost at the same time in August 1940 when Veltjens began his negotiations in Helsinki. The group intended as the inheritors of the Jaeger tradition was established on the 12th March 1941 i.e. a year after the Winter War had ended and three months before Germany attacked the Soviet Union. Because it was attached to the Waffen-SS formations of the Nazi Party and not to the regular military force as Finns had hoped, it received emphasized political significance. Germany wanted to stress the political character of her multi-national troops. Most of the foreigners served in SS units.

Waffen-SS swore their military allegiance to Hitler personally. This formally personal relationship to Hitler was the only factor that joined the political SS and the SS troops manning the concentration camps with the Finnish SS battalion. Thus the Finnish volunteers who went to Germany had an even worse reputation than they deserved.

Initially the battalion had 1 100 recruits. They were surprisingly young; nearly half of them were under the legal recruitment age. Many of them did not decide to go to Germany and war from ideological convictions. The probable incentive was the same as it had been for many Jaegers – the romance of war and the need for adventure. Of course the political attitudes of the men in the battalion leaned to the right but not as much as the Germans would have wished. It appears that only about 20 per cent of them could be classified as right wing radicals.

The Finnish SS battalion was no show unit of the German propaganda war. The Germans sent them to the front with no pity. The Finns fought in the southern flank of Germany's Eastern Front and by spring 1943 they had advanced across the Don to the Caucasus. The Finnish SS men paid dearly for their desire for adventure. In the course of a couple of years over 1 400 men served in the battalion, about 270 of them fell or were missing in action. Nearly half of them were wounded. The battalion's overall losses in relative terms were about three times as high as the losses of the Finnish army during the same period.

The battalion was an important political gesture from the Finns and on Finland's scale a fairly sizable transfer of manpower to Germany. The Finns believed that this sacrifice would yield political benefit but the trouble taken and the losses suffered did not correspond to the benefit gained. To the Germans, one Finnish battalion meant the same as hundreds and thousands of other battalions.

Establishing the Finnish SS battalion did not achieve the goals that were set for it. It had to be disbanded in spring 1943 in a very difficult situation. The political risk that emerged in conjunction with disbanding it was much greater than the small propaganda benefit obtained initially.

Driftwood or Not?

Finland began to rush towards a new war in spring 1941. The political leadership in Helsinki had front row seats from which to follow this fierce development. Germany attempted to be politically as inconspicuous as possible so as not to reveal her wild intentions before the time was ripe. Undoubtedly Hitler pressed for his three-nation agreement and military presence in the direction of the Balkans. It could be interpreted as the finishing touches of the Western operations the previous spring. It soon emerged that it was the overture to the military campaign in the East.

From at least the end of May 1941 onwards, the Finns saw that something significant was in the making. The invitation of the delegation of officers to Germany and the discussions there showed that Europe was entering a totally new phase. Finland was formally cautious and attempted to present a neutral facade but she saw a great opportunity approaching.

In early June 1941 the government sent a message to the Germans that Finland did not want to attack. But it knew that had it withdrawn it would have had to bury all its hopes concerning Karelia. Therefore the Finns behaved differently from the way they spoke. They continued to affirm their neutrality but acted like comrades-in-arms. Gradually Finland slid into the wake of the aggressor so that she would not have to make the decisive move but that she could reap all the benefits from the situation when Hitler made his move.

As early as two weeks before Operation Barbarossa, German offensive troops arrived in Finland. A week before Hitler's D-day German mine-layers and submarines began to operate in Finland's territorial waters, a German liaison

May 1941

Territory of Germany and
its Allies

Territory conquered by
the Soviet Union

The starting points for the battle between dictators
emerged in spring 1941. Germany spread towards the
Balkans and the Soviet Union occupied Bessarabia. In
this configuration Finland had to decide on her attitude towards Germany's attack on the Soviet Union.
Previous map on page 28.
Following map on page 57.

officer with the rank of General arrived in the country, and Mannerheim attached the troops in northern Finland to the command of the Germans. Finland mobilized her army once and for all on 17th June 1941, four days before Germany's official announcement of her attack.

Throughout the post-war period it has been disputed whether Finland was a calculating aggressor or a piece of driftwood in whirling rapids. Both descriptions are clearly correct.

Finland's desire to attack can not be covered up by the fact that she expected the opposition to hit first. She had announced in advance that she would participate in the war as soon as there was a suitable reason. From this perspective Finland was the aggressor.

However, Finland would never have arrived at this situation that it secretly hoped for, unless Hitler had begun his great Eastern campaign. The decision that led Finland into launching the offensive in summer 1941 was not made in Helsinki but in Berlin. Hitler was the aggressor. Finland availed of the aggressor's unscrupulousness and camouflaged her actions so carefully that she began to believe in her own innocence.

What Did Finland Want?

The most important political goal of the Continuation War was to regain what Finland had lost in the Winter War. This goal was already set in secret discussions by the government on the last day of the Winter War. The German attack on the Soviet Union in summer 1941 created a totally new situation. Finland could not refrain from examining the possibility that she would win more than she had lost.

It was part of Germany's bluffing tactics in May-June 1941 to go through the motions that she was seriously conducting military and political negotiations with the Soviet Union. The Ryti government received a vaguely formulated question as to what it thought of the future arrangement of the country's Eastern border. The General Headquarters began feverishly to study different alternatives. The summer 1939 situation threatened to repeat itself. The Finns wanted absolutely to avoid the situation where negotiations were carried out over their heads once again.

The military plans started from the premise that the Finnish-Soviet border on the Karelian Isthmus should be redrawn because of the security of Leningrad. They proposed acquiring territorial compensation on the northern side of Lake Ladoga. But they also emphasized that the routes that were vital to the Soviet Union should be left free.

The most cautious alternative was outlined for the event that Hitler and Stalin would again solve their dispute through negotiations. However, the situation would be different in the event of war between Germany and the Soviet Union. Then the Finns would want to push the eastern border 400 kilometres further into the Soviet Union along the line running from the south-eastern tip of Lake Ladoga through the bottom of Lake Onega to the White Sea. The idea was to create the wildernesses north of Lake Ladoga into a buffer zone which would give Finland the opportunity of concentrating most of her army in the Isthmus. The loftiest plans were removed at the last moment from Finland's official list of wishes. In the document sent to Germany the government only wished to regain the territories lost in the Winter War, guarantees for the country's borders, foodstuffs and German support for the questions of nickel and water power disputed with the Soviet Union.

A dream of much further-reaching goals, however, lingered on well into the Continuation War. The formal policy of the Ryti government was subdued and cautious. But behind the scenes it was forced to wrestle with the problems of political realism and national romantic castles in the air. And it did not always know itself which side it was on.

FINLAND JOINS IN

The Continuation War started as wars usually start. Both parties announced that they had begun the war because the opponent had opened fire.

Who Shot First?

Finland's politics was based on the idea that she would not look like the aggressor although she was participating in Hitler's attack. The Finns hoped to be provoked and the Soviets tried not to provoke. However, the situation was hopeless because the military force of a state which had attacked the Soviet Union was on Finnish soil and which cared nothing for the shadow boxing between Finland and the Soviet Union.

Finland's records were not as clean as the official orders show. Prime Minister Jukka Rangell said in Parliament on 25th June 1941 that Finland was again at war because the Soviet Union had opened fire; early in the morning of the 25th June Soviet planes had attacked 19 targets on Finnish soil.

However, Finnish submarines had been laying mines together with German vessels in the Gulf of Finland three days before the bombings, i.e. on the day Hitler attacked. From the beginning of the war onwards, the Germans used two airfields in southern Finland for the bombers bound for the Soviet Union and this naturally happened with Finnish permission. On the first day of the war German planes bombed the Soviet base in Hanko.

The Soviet Union had started limited warfare against Finland on the first day of Operation Barbarossa. Its planes bombed Finnish battleships and there was also intermittent firing on border areas. However, these conflicts were not the political provocation that the Finns wished for. The large scale Soviet air raid on 25th June was almost a relief to Finland. Without it she would have had to continue the very peculiar situation of falling between two stools; to play neutral and yet submit to being a base for a great power at war.

If it is absolutely necessary to find a scapegoat for starting the war, it is obviously Finland. The Soviet Union did shoot first but Finland had engaged in military action before this. However, finding the scapegoat is not at all important historically and politically. In the last few days of June no strength on earth could have kept Finland's Eastern border untouched by war.

"Scabbard" Order of the Day

When Finland attacked Mannerheim gave his famous order of the day on 10th July 1941. In it he repeated his pledge that he had given in February 1918, during the Civil War, that he would not scabbard his sword before he had freed the Soviet territories populated by a Finno-Ugrian people in Eastern Karelia. He said that a new day had dawned and that the freedom of Karelia and great Finland was glimpsed in this historical tide.

The order of the day was a considerable shock to the Social Democrats in particular but also to all others who had not internalized the concept of a Greater Finland and eastern Karelian irredenta. The Social Democrats and Communists too did agree to fight to regain the Karelian Isthmus but acquiring extra territory beyond the old border was a different matter. It aroused great opposition, particularly since Mannerheim's order of the day linked it to the left wing's gloomy year of 1918.

The preparations for this order of the day had been going on in Mannerheim's headquarters in Mikkeli for a couple of weeks, i.e. since the beginning of the war. It was still a surprise to the government. Greater Finland as such was known to almost all ministers but they too understood that an open declaration of intentions for expansion would harm Finland's reputation abroad and would put the country's internal unity to the test.

The inner circles criticized Mannerheim for setting far-reaching goals for Finnish politics without negotiations with the government. The Marshall defended himself on very formal grounds and said that the order of the day did not speak of Greater Finland but of great Finland and these were two different things. In addition Mannerheim said that the Commander-in-Chief must have the freedom to encourage his troops to fight. He calmly announced that the military leader himself always decides how this is done at any given moment.

The Social Democrat ministers of the government threatened to resign. Defence Minister Rudolf Walden who had been taken into the government as Mannerheim's trustee offered to take responsibility and resign. He had seen drafts for the order of the day in advance, but did not take the matter up with the government. However, nobody dared to put Mannerheim's authority publicly to the test. The order of the day became part of the official facade of Finnish politics although behind the scenes the government de facto dissociated itself from it.

The government adopted an officially softened version of the programme of objectives declared by Mannerheim. It began to repeat the phrase that Finland was fighting a defensive war. The aim of securing as safe a border as possible could lead to crossing the old Eastern border. Mannerheim's great Finland declaration based on the pledge of his sword was compensated for with a political slogan: short borders – long lasting peace.

A Separate War

The point of departure for Finland's official doctrine of security policy was that the country was waging a separate war. It did not have a binding alliance with Germany under international law. The only uniting factor was a common enemy. Finland decided herself on her military operations and chose her political line independently of Germany.

Fundamentally what was involved was that Finland was trying to exploit the fluctuating politics of Europe for the achievement of her own limited goals. In the early stages of the war the goal was to regain the territory she had lost but from mid-summer 1941 onwards it was the conquering of foreign territory.

The Soviet Union officially treated Finland as she did any of Hitler's allies. However, Stalin's actions indicate that he understood in part Finland's claims that she was waging a separate war or at least he considered Finland politically the weakest link in Hitler's front. As early as the beginning of August 1941, i.e. when the war had been going on for less than two months, the Soviet Union announced to the Western Powers that she aimed at a separate peace with Finland. The United States conveyed this message to Helsinki but it did not interest the Finns who were intoxicated by their good progress in the offensive.

Stalin's hint at the possibility of peace at this stage already was significant, though it led nowhere. First of all it showed how desperate the Soviet situation was. It also showed that Stalin considered Finland militarily so important that he would have been willing to bargain considerably his political principles in order to achieve immediate military benefit. The Finnish claim of the separate nature of their war was better understood in Moscow than the Finns noticed or believed. After all Stalin proposed a separate peace in a war that the Finns claimed was indeed a separate war.

Although Finland ignored Stalin's initiative the Western Powers continued to put pressure on Helsinki. In her strongly worded notes and serious discussions, the United States conveyed her understanding that Finland was on the wrong side and should immediately detach herself from the war.

According to United States representatives Finland could never base her security on a line running along the isthmuses from the Gulf of Finland to the White Sea. Security could only be guaranteed by constructing good political relations and an atmosphere of trust between Finland and the Soviet Union. After the war Finland heeded this advice but in autumn 1941 this good counsel fell on deaf ears.

The Price of the Offensive

The offensive of the Continuation War looked splendid. Finland rapidly proceeded from one victory to another and seemed in a moment to fulfill the dreams of even the wildest national romantics. Yet, not even a very successful offensive is a parade. The reality of war is always blood and mud.

During the five-month offensive Finland lost over 25 000 men, nearly 4 000 more than it did in the Winter War. The sacrifice of the Winter War had seemed intolerably great but the even greater losses in the early months of the Continuation War hardly carried political weight in official statements. It was visible in village cemeteries and was felt in individual families. The rows of heroes' graves grew longer. The regional system applied in mobilization concentrated the losses in bunches to those districts whose units ended up in the worst spots in battles. Bloodletting hit the most vulnerable part, from the point of view of regenerating the population, 20 to 30 year-old men.

At the beginning of the war Finland literally mobilized all her strength. Towards the end of June 1941 the overall strength of the army was 470 000 men i.e. about 13 per cent of the population. When citizens who were ordered to posts indirectly connected with the war are included, the mobilization percentage rises to about 16, which was probably among the highest figures in the Second World War. Demographically the war was already total.

An almost complete mobilization was a heavy

burden on Finland's economy. Important work was left undone. Some of the grain was left in the fields in the autumn because there were not enough people to harvest it. There was a shortage of firewood because forestry workers were at the front.

The Continuation War began in a spirit of general enthusiasm. Everybody wanted the territories lost in the Winter War back. The moment of truth came when this target was achieved and the troops proceeded across the old Eastern border. The first refusals to continue took place in July 1941 on the Karelian Isthmus. But they were mostly prompted by physical exhaustion after the zealous period of attack. In early September, refusal to fight became more common and political stands were discernible. Insubordination by soldiers rose to the level that it affected operations in conjunction with crossing the river by troops that had penetrated furthest East. The first attack failed because the troops did not obey orders.

The troops that had advanced to East Karelia had more serious disciplinary problems than those on the Isthmus. The problem worsened the deeper into East Karelia the troops advanced and the worse were the fighting conditions.

However, insubordination did not reach such heights that it affected the army's ability to fight; there were some 500 objectors in an army of slightly less than 500 000 and most of them changed their minds after a reprimand. Even after the reprimands there were still slightly under 200 objectors and the commanders took a harder line. Court-martials sentenced four soldiers to death from among the objectors of autumn 1941. Two of them were carried out. Additionally a hundred or so men were sentenced to hard labour lasting from three to ten years.

Tanner's Line

The Social Democratic Party found itself in a difficult situation when the offensive ended. The Communists and the left-wing Social Democrats had been imprisoned soon after war broke out. The Social Democratic Party majority now alone represented the opinion opposing the crossing of the Eastern border. Yet its representatives sat in the government that was at war beyond the Eastern border.

The Party Chairman Väinö Tanner was the Minister for Trade and Industry but he played a much greater role in the government than his position implied. He had to play a difficult double role. He loyally represented the government's policy to the outside world but presented critical views of his party within it.

In the course of the autumn Tanner's public speeches began to contain reservations but he used very careful wording so as not to show fractions in the united front. He demanded that the advancement should be stopped at some "reasonable" line. As early as mid-September 1941 when the Eastern Karelian operation was still badly incomplete he said that Finland had achieved her most important goals in the war.

In late autumn the government set out to decide on the administration of the occupied area. On 25th November 1941, Tanner sent a long letter full of warnings to President Ryti. He said that Finland could keep East Karelia only if the Soviet Union was finally crushed in the war. However, Tanner did not consider that likely because "a nation of 200 million cannot be wiped from the face of the earth just like that".

Tanner further pointed out that the Soviet Union's grounds for demands concerning the Karelian Isthmus during the Winter War had the same logic that Finland used for her operations in East Karelia. He warned that the occupied East Karelia would become an economic burden to Finland as colonies had always been to their mother country. After the war Tanner acquired for himself the reputation of a political hot-head but in the fever of the Continuation War he was able to keep a much cooler head than many others.

An Agreement to Please Hitler

Even before the major war, in November 1936, Germany and Japan concluded an Anti-Comintern Pact. It expired at the end of 1941. Germany wanted to make a show of renewing it and began to gather new signatories.

The Helsinki government said that joining this kind of agreement would be rather harmless politically. An anti-Communist declaration in principle would not mean much for Finland had shown her attitude to Communism in practice in the Winter War. Signing a secondary document would reduce the danger of becoming involved in an arrangement that would be even more burdening politically.

Just before these negotiations Finland had to ask Germany to sell 175 000 tons of grain; otherwise the country's food supplies would have run out during the winter. The Helsinki government had to choose between hunger and the indignation of the Western States. It decided to submit to this indignation.

Finland hoped to come through the signing ceremony of the Anti-Comintern Pact on 25th November 1941 quietly and with as little political damage as possible. This was not to be, however. Foreign Minister Rolf Witting noticed first of all that he had ended up in a group of third-class powers. He was beside the representatives of Slovakia, Croatia and China's Nanking. Other new signitories were Denmark, Romania and Bulgaria. Finland was the star of the ceremony. The hero of the Winter War and the conqueror of East Karelia was the only new signatory to the pact with military proof of anti-Communist action. Hitler's Germany appreciated this and now Finland had to suffer for it politically.

Ultimately on the Wrong Side

Finland's participation in Hitler's attack aroused surprise and bitterness in Britain. The goodwill capital acquired during the Winter War lost a great deal of its nominal value in a moment. The political significance of the remaining goodwill disappeared into thin air, for Finland's enemy was Britain's ally.

Hitler was discontent with Finnish attempts to avoid a public breakdown in relations with Britain by all possible means. By contrast, Stalin put pressure on Britain because she maintained relations with the enemy of the Soviet Union. The Germans and some Finns believed that the British Embassy in Helsinki could acquire military and political information that was immediately relayed to the Soviet Union to the detriment of both Finland and Germany.

The breaking off of relations with Britain was inevitable but Finland wanted it to look like a British initiative. Diplomatic relations were severed only at the end of July 1941 after the British airforce had bombed Petsamo. However, this was only half a solution.

In autumn 1941, Hitler put pressure on Fin-

December 1941

Territory of Germany and
its Allies

In December 1941 the German army was in the
suburbs of Moscow. Finland had occupied East Karelia and had entered into the Anti-Comintern Pact. Ryti
and Mannerheim gave an evasive response to Britain's
demands for curbing warfare and she declared war on
Finland.

Previous map on page 43.
Following map on page 73.

land to intensify her political relations with Germany. At the same time Britain encouraged her to move in exactly the opposite direction. She demanded that Helsinki cease hostilities against the Soviet Union.

When Finland signed the Anti-Comintern Pact, Britain presented her with an ultimatum. If Finland would not halt her attack by 3rd December 1941, Britain would declare war on her. Prime Minister Winston Churchill personally contacted Mannerheim and appealed to him to stop the offensive.

In their replies the Finns emphasized that their intention was merely to regain the territories lost in the Winter War and secure the safety of the country's borders. Neither the government nor Mannerheim announced that the Marshal had already given the command to cease attack after Finland had conquered Karhumäki. Thus Finland was acting in the way Britain demanded but failed to report it. Since the replies to London did not contain the promise demanded of them, Britain declared war on Finland on her independence day, 6th December 1941.

Britain mastered diplomacy better than Finland. The exchange of notes that led to the declaration of war made the configuration look as though Britain's decision stemmed not so much from Stalin's pressure as it did from the excessive enthusiasm for the offensive displayed by the Finns. The inevitable result came in the very way that the Finns had tried to avoid in every possible way.

THE LULL
IN THE WAR

Comparing Hitler's speeches with his de facto advancement in the Russian campaign as early as autumn 1941 showed that the blitzkrieg was no longer the same kind of brilliant show as the occupation of France had been. Mannerheim was able to interpret the advancement of the German offensive better than most other Finns. He examined it from a soldier's perspective and had personal knowledge of the geographical conditions in which Germany attacked – he had received his military training in Czarist Russia. As early as the end of 1941, Mannerheim began to suspect the possibility of Hitler's victory.

Mannerheim and Hitler

The Marshal's thinking was decisively influenced by the fact that the Soviet Union was able to regain the town of Tikhvin, 200 kilometres east of Leningrad in December 1941. It ultimately cut off the advancement of German troops on the Eastern side of Lake Ladoga and prevented them from contacting the Finnish troops that had advanced to the river Svir in the North-Eastern corner of Lake Ladoga. Mannerheim put the brakes on the war. He wanted to save Finland's strength and avoid politically sensitive manoeuvres.

During the trench warfare the Germans suggested a joint offensive on the Murmansk railway line on several occasions. Mannerheim juggled his words in such a way as to seem to always give a positive reply but usually gave the condition that the Germans achieve something visible in Leningrad, in the direction of Svir or on its Eastern front. Mannerheim had the upper hand in this military diplomacy. He could say with innocent factualism that the Finns were on the river Svir waiting for their comrades-in-arms who could be neither seen nor heard.

It was a questionable honour for Finland that Hitler came to congratulate Mannerheim on his 75th birthday in June 1942. It was a non-political courtesy visit but still a very conspicuous propaganda gesture that created an impression of close alliance. For courtesy reasons Mannerheim had to make a reciprocal visit to Germany.

These visits seemed to emphasize Finland's contacts with Germany. On the other hand it was unthinkable that Hitler would visit the commander-in-chief of a vassal state. Vassals come to see their masters. Thus in principle this visit can be interpreted as an indication that Finland still retained her own political springboard. This view remained noticed only by those Finns who heroically tried to invent a positive explanation to this embarrassing series of events.

Diplomatic Front

Soon after Britain had declared war on Finland, Foreign Minister, Anthony Eden, negotiated in Moscow the new situation that had emerged after Japan had attacked Pearl Harbour. Surprisingly, Stalin proposed a secret agreement according to which the Allies would define the Western border of the Soviet Union. Stalin's proposal would have given Finland back the border negotiated at the end of the Winter War. Additionally he said that he would demand a base and a military agreement of Finland. Britain refused to make bilateral arrangements that a General Peace Conference to be held after the war would decide.

Later in the spring Britain's opposition began to waver. Churchill was prepared to bend to Stalin's demands. He felt that it was not sensible to put into jeopardy the interests of the Empire because of a few small eastern European states. However the United States' President, Franklin D. Roosevelt, remained unyielding. He announced that the United States would publicly denounce the agreement between Britain and the Soviet Union if the agreement took a stance on border questions. Stalin gave way. Britain and the Soviet Union signed their agreement of alliance in May 1942 but it did not define the Western border of the Soviet Union. Hence it did not make a stand on the position of Finland either.

However, the negotiations had shown to the West what Stalin wanted. His proposals did not seem to threaten Finland's independence. This increased the United States' desire to get Helsinki and Moscow at least to discuss the possibility of peace. But its explorations did not extend to contacts between the countries. Thus in the diplomacy of the European War the idea of a separate peace for Finland lingered on although Helsinki had turned it down in the autumn.

At the same time Europe's military configuration changed decisively and Finland's position became easier, at least in principle. In April 1942 Hitler decided that the oil from the Caucasus was the strategic solution to the war. Despite the opposition of his military leaders, he ordered that Germany's military power be focussed in the South on 5th April 1942. At the same time as he ordered a major attack in the South he gave the Northern Front the task of occupying Leningrad. Not many knew that it was a secondary goal, however.

Had Hitler continued to focus his operations on political and industrial centres in the Soviet Union, the situation in Leningrad would have become even worse than it now did. Finland too would then have become more entangled in Germany's offensive and through this her politics, too. Hitler's decision to transfer the focus to the south freed the Finns from this discomfort.

The Occupation of East Karelia

The Finns presented themselves as the liberators and national benefactors of the Finnish areas of East Karelia. However, the population there took a different attitude. This is the way the occupied always behaved to the occupier; indifferently if they were left in peace and with hostility if they were put under pressure.

The first surprise the occupiers got was that East Karelia was nearly empty. The pre-war population of the area beyond the old Eastern border occupied by Finland was about 300 000 but only 85 000 during the occupation. It appears that the population of Finnish origin followed the evacuation order by the Soviet authorities just as obediently as the Russians.

Indeed the occupiers were kin to the Karelians. Nonetheless in the eyes of the local population they were intruders. The well-meaning enthusiasm of the Finns did not receive a warm welcome. The antagonism increased. Some of the East Karelians did not understand Finnish despite their linguistic relationship. The Finns began to teach them Finnish. The radio of the occupied administration adopted a linguistic policy aimed at getting rid of the local dialect. Attempts to convert the Orthodox population to Lutherism were carried out through force at times. The non-Finno-Ugrian population was herded onto isolation camps.

The occupiers' administration was not as humane as one could expect from national romantics. It was mostly cultural imperialism, work carried out at the condition of Finnishness to make East Karelians Finnish. It was not a particularly praiseworthy policy of nationalism, for it alienated East Karelians from the Finns. But the well-meaning basic tone of the Finnish occupier made the daily life of the East Karelians easier. The grip of the occupiers' administration was clumsy but its sincere goal was to persuade the population into becoming Finnish. That is why its grip was as gentle as that of an occupier's administration can be.

Had the East Karelian people felt spiritually Finnish, they would presumably have followed the occupiers when in summer 1944 they withdrew from East Karelia. Only three per cent of the population of the occupied area "voted with their feet". More than 80 000 East Karelians remained to await the arrival of the Soviet troops in the final stages of the war in the same way that they had remained to await the arrival of the Finns three years earlier.

Following Hitler's visit to Finland in summer 1942 the next high-ranking German visitor was the head of the SS, Heinrich Himmler, who supervised the concentration camps and extermination centres. They were systematically implementing Hitler's order given in January 1942 on the final solution of the question of European Jews.

The Finns schemed to prevent the Jewish question from becoming a concrete issue during Himmler's visit. This tactical victory in evasion did not help much. The discussion shifted from political to administrative affairs and this worsened the situation. In the course of autumn 1942 the extradition to Germany of refugees residing in Finland was dealt with like any police administrative arrangement whatsoever.

By November 1942 Finland extradited to Germany a total of 77 refugees of whom eight were Jews. Extraditions were normally based on criminal charges, which were all insignificantly small misdemeanors and some were totally without grounds. They ended because the fate of the Jews caused a domestic policy storm. Censorship allowed the publication of news concerning the extradition question and the Social Democrats made it into a public scandal.

The Prime Minister and the Minister of the Interior, whose administrative sphere it came under, were out of town when the news hit the headlines. The Minister of Finance, Väinö Tanner, gave the secret police the order to discontinue extraditions until the government had handled the question. This took place on 3rd November 1942 in a session in which there were no minutes kept. Obviously the government decided to ban mass extraditions and that each case would have to be examined separately.

In spite of everything one more dispatch of refugees was put into German hands after the government decision, but these 27 people were the last refugees extradited from Finland to Germany. This group also included all the Jews surrendered during the war. They were sent to Auschwitz and only one of them survived.

Extraditions were not based on actual political pressure by a Great Power. Surprisingly they ended after Himmler's visit in summer 1942. Neither were they based on race. They were based on the petty Finnish police authorities' desire to ingratiate themselves with their German colleagues.

In addition to this, the question of extradition also indicated the strength and preparedness of the Finnish democratic system, even under exceptional conditions. Censorship notwithstanding, the press could operate as a state guard dog and sever the chain of events which would have otherwise become a moral millstone around the nation's neck.

There were about 1 500 Jews in Finland during the wars. About 300 of them fought in the army alongside other Finnish citizens and 23 of them fell. Not a single Finnish Jew was extradited to Germany. The Finnish policy concerning Jews was blameless during the war but the policy on refugees was blemished.

Censorship of the press was fumbling and indecisive in the early stages of the Continuation War. It shows that Finland did not commit herself in advance to Hitler's Barbarossa operation. Cen-

Censored Finland

sorship would have been brightly polished in the spring if Finland's decision to join the war had been planned as carefully and as far in advance as the German offensive.

After the immediate initial chaos of the war the government was able to use censorship rather skillfully. The press reported on the Anti-Comintern Pact and Britain's declaration of war on Finland mostly along the lines that the government had defined and that were advantageous to it.

Problems emerged when the government had decided to make peace their main goal but had to ward off public discussion of the matter. It was through the Swedish press that the actions of the peace opposition became public. At times it also became visible in the Finnish press, but it was mainly forced to report on the reasons for which a separate peace was not possible, stressing the attitude defined by the government.

Relations between the press and its censors were surprisingly balanced. It appears that the great majority of leading journalists saw the sense in censorship. They wanted to follow the official security policy line and stayed on course as long as the war lasted.

In fact political changes are discernible in the guidelines for censorship earlier than in other governmental action. As early as in autumn 1942, Germany's opposition notwithstanding, the Finnish press began to report on the progress of the war based on information from Western sources with as little fuss as possible. The idea was to prepare the public for the fact that the war would not last for ever and that a German defeat could not be excluded. Naturally the press could not mediate a very realistic picture of the progress of the war. When explorations for the possibility of peace were really launched in spring 1944 censorship was tightened to its extreme.

Yet public opinion was not quite so unprepared for peace as it had been at the end of the Winter War. The press mediated the most important information on the chaos of the situation on the Karelian Isthmus in summer 1944 and on the rapid deterioration of the German military position. It showed that peace was inevitable.

Censorship can not be avoided when arms do the talking, and when censorship works democracy does not. However, the press during the Continuation War was not quite without teeth. It could put an end to the extradition of Jewish refugees to Germany and to report on the existence of anti-government peace movements. For the press in a country at war Finland's was exceptionally free for the most part. Although democracy was put under blinds it still remained a democracy.

The Finns' old acquaintance Boris Yartsev was a Legation Secretary in Stockholm during the Continuation War. At the end of October 1942 he told the Social Democratic journalist, Richard Lindström, that the Soviet Union could negotiate a separate peace with Finland. He considered the 1939 borders as a basis for starting explorations for peace and hinted that the Western Powers might guarantee Finland's borders.

Lindström hurriedly relayed the message to the Finns but the government in Helsinki decided that attempts at negotiations could not be made on that basis. Yartsev's proposal which was meant to be enticing was not enticing enough; the

**Finland Begins
to Falter**

67

Finns held large areas east of the border line offered to them obscurely.

Yartsev's message was also suspect because it was in conflict with the information filtered to Helsinki about Eden's negotiations in Moscow the previous spring. At that time Stalin had clearly demanded the 1940 borders and much more from Finland. Yartsev's unofficial exploration began to look like an attempt to draw Finland onto thin ice. The breakdown in negotiations could then be blamed on Finland and would poison the already problematic relations with the United States.

Yartsev's initiative was almost shrugged off but it did have its own significance. Major things seemed to be in the pipeline in the Great War. General Erwin Rommel, the great German war hero, had suffered a stinging defeat at El Alamein in November 1942, the Allies had landed in North Africa on 8th November 1942 and Germany's attack on Stalingrad in December 1942 had become bogged down.

Ryti was of two minds. But his 1942 Independence Day speech followed the official line. It pacified Berlin but angered Washington once and for all. But there were signs of change in the air. The Germans had many causes for concern and one of them was what the Finns thought of the whole war deep down.

FINLAND
DECIDES

Hitler's generals had opposed the shifting of the war's main emphasis to Southern Russia and they were right. It forced Germany to concentrate hundreds and thousands of men in the Volga area almost beyond reach of maintenance. The moment of truth dawned in Stalingrad at the end of 1942, beginning of 1943. In September 1942 Germany had captured the main sections of the city. Towards the end of November the Soviet Union commenced a massive counter-attack and encircled the 250 000 strong German army in Stalingrad. After a painful and tenacious battle the last Germans surrendered at the beginning of February 1943.

The battle for Stalingrad was a military turning point but it was also a psychological breakthrough. The Germans, considered invincible, had been beaten so spectacularly that no official explanation could hide the truth any longer. Field Marshal Friedrich Paulus, the commander-in-chief of the army attacking Stalingrad, 24 Generals and almost 100 000 Germans were made prisoners of war in the Soviet Union. In the course of the autumn the Western Allies achieved

**Stalingrad
and Leningrad**

a spectacular victory when British troops drove General Erwin Rommel's forces out of North Africa.

At the same time a turning point took place on the Leningrad front which influenced Finland's military and political position even more directly than Stalingrad. The forces breaking out of the encircled city opened up a strip less than ten kilometres wide towards the shore of Lake Ladoga which improved the logistics situation in Leningrad. However, German artillery was able to disrupt the supply lines and the vital railway link remained in German hands.

Simultaneously with the Soviet Union's spectacular military initiative the Western Allies strengthened their political grip in a manner that caused concern to Finns. In January 1943 Churchill and Roosevelt held a summit meeting in Casablanca. In the press conference held at the end of it Roosevelt announced that the Allies had decided to demand unconditional surrender of the Axle states. The wording sounded ominous. It appeared to indicate that the Allies would make no difference between Germany and the states that fought alongside her.

Finland was rapidly sliding down a military and political slippery slope. The theory of a separate war was no longer marketable internationally. As soon as possible it would have to be changed into a separate peace. Otherwise the consequences would be bad for Finland.

Peace Becomes Target of War

The turning point in the war placed Finland's leaders under new kinds of pressures. Hitler's fate turned towards defeat but Germany still remained so strong that breaking loose was not possible just like that. Finland had to play a difficult double game between her enemy and her comrade-in-arms to secure her own interests.

In addition to the turning point on the general political scene, Finland experienced a domestic crisis. Ryti's presidential term of office came to an end on 1st March 1943. His re-election was a political certainty but approaching presidential elections gave an opportunity to change the government and political course. Finland's political continuity was so strong that the old government defined the task for its successor. Before the presidential election Mannerheim had already invited Ryti and his war cabinet to his headquarters, which were a couple of hundred kilometres to the North-East of Helsinki, to discuss the impact of Stalingrad and Leningrad on Finland's position. Their unanimous conclusion was that Finland had ended up on the losing side and therefore she would have to disengage herself from the war before fateful political damage was done.

Creating normal relations based on trust with the Soviet Union was set as a goal. If the price for peace included giving up East Karelia it would have to be done. However, this line of practical politics was drawn cautiously because oil and grain came from Germany and there were no other suppliers in sight. Tearing an open rift with Germany would have meant a jump into the dark. Apart from cold and hunger everything else would be uncertain. Therefore it was decided to aim for peace primarily in mutual understanding with Germany.

It was almost foolhardy to scheme to buy peace by giving up East Karelia. A dear price had been paid in blood and suffering for this conquered area. Public opinion was not ripe to give it up without a fight. Mannerheim, Ryti and the government's inner circle convening in Mikkeli took personal political risks by starting to pursue a policy that they considered right but against public opinion.

After the presidential election Ryti appointed the Conservative Edwin Linkomies, a professor in classical languages, who had been the second speaker in Parliament, as the new Prime Minister. Rolf Witting, who was accused of having German leanings, had to give up his position as Foreign Minister and he was replaced by Henrik Ramsay who had been the Minister of Supply in the previous government. He had good relations with Anglo Saxon business circles thanks to having been in the shipping trade.

The appointment of the new government gave a clear signal: Finland had decided to make peace but not under any conditions whatsoever.

Attempts by the United States

Soon after the Casablanca meeting it appeared that the Soviet Union did not intend to apply the principle of unconditional surrender to Finland. The Soviet Ambassador, Maxim Litvinov, explained to the U.S. Foreign Minister, Cordell Hull, that Moscow considered it natural that the Baltic States belonged to the Soviet Union but Finland was in a different position. The Kremlin wanted to see it as "a healthy, independent state". He said that peace could be concluded on the basis of the situation that existed after the Winter War.

It was just what the United States' leadership wanted to hear. It immediately offered its services as a mediator to launch peace negotiations be-

April 1943

Territory of Germany and
its Allies

Territory conquered by
the Soviet Union

In spring 1943 Finland explored the possibilities for peace for the first time seriously. Germany had suffered a militarily and psychologically decisive defeat in Stalingrad but remained strong. Finland tried to detach herself from her partner in war through negotiations and had to learn that a civilized breaking off of relations with Hitler was not possible.

Previous map on page 57.
Following map on page 85.

tween Finland and the Soviet Union. Linkomies' peace government took the offer seriously.

The new Foreign Minister, Ramsay, was sent to Berlin to examine how to break up with Germany in a civilized manner. The trip turned out to be a total catastrophe. Ramsay was inundated with accusations of betrayal and threats of occupation. The childish attempt by the Finns taught them a lesson they would not forget: too much honesty is bad in war.

While Ramsay was sent to Berlin the government asked Washington to get precise information on the conditions of peace which Moscow envisaged. Molotov immediately presented them to the U.S. Ambassador to Moscow, and Washington was surprised. The conditions were much harsher than expected. Molotov said that the Peace Treaty of Moscow concluded after the Winter War should enter into force in its entirety, but this was no longer enough for the Soviet Union. Relations with Germany would have to be severed immediately, the army would have to be demobilized at once and Finland would have to pay reparations for half the damage she had caused.

The United States leadership felt that the conditions were so harsh that it would be pointless to go on mediating on that basis. She withdrew her services announcing that she had not offered to be a mediator but tried only to create the basis for negotiations. Finland, for her part, felt that Moscow had failed to present an agenda for negotiations. So there was nothing to negotiate about.

The first serious attempt to contact the Soviet Union brought about more damage than the failed attempt. The United States received information on Ramsay's trip to Berlin. It seemed to prove that Finland was Germany's direct vassal. Finland's relations with the United States became intense in the extreme.

The exploration for the possibility of peace was the carefully guarded secret of the closed inner circle. The political elite outside the government had no tangible information on peace attempts. Parliament had the idea that the government was doing nothing although the European war was developing in a worse and worse direction. Groups were formed within the government and among the Swedish-speaking intelligentsia, demanding efficiency and speed for the peace process. Towards the end of August the peace opposition delivered an address to Ryti signed by 33 important political figures calling for a speedy settlement, i.e. the very target pursued by the Linkomies government.

The signatories of the address did not want to harm the myth of the unity of the home front. They intended to keep the document in confidence. However, it was leaked to the press in Stockholm. The government had been aware of the address in advance and did not oppose it as such. Finland's credibility in negotiations could improve if the enemy saw that there was a non-communist trend of opinion for peace, loyal to the government in Finland. However, the situation was different after the address became public. It began to look like the politics of protest and gave the impression of fractures in Finland's domestic front.

At the beginning of September the government

The Race between the Government and the Peace Opposition

gave Parliament a foreign policy report which was discussed in a secret session. In these discussions Linkomies announced bluntly that the government's aim was the same as the peace opposition's although it could not be proclaimed everywhere.

The joint aims of the government and peace opposition found no response in Moscow but created a reaction in Berlin that the Finns would have liked to avoid to the very end. Straight after the catastrophe in Stalingrad, the German leadership noted that the Finnish morale was ebbing and it began to call for a political union to strengthen the relationship of comrades-in-arms. The Finns made a fast series of diplomatic evasions and the Germans withdrew their demand. Linkomies' festive phraseology in a war heroes' memorial on 16th May 1943 was accepted as a guarantee of Finnish faithfulness.

In autumn 1943 the cards were put on the table. Germany once again demanded an official alliance agreement and Finland warded it off just as officially with no excuses. It was explained to Ribbentrop that the Finnish Parliament would never approve this kind of an agreement and that was that.

Stalin Dictates Towards the end of October 1943 the foreign ministers of the three great powers, the US., Britain and the Soviet Union prepared in Moscow the first summit of the Allies. The foreign ministers agreed on many important issues from the viewpoint of peace settlements. The Allies agreed that the main responsibility for negotiations for a truce and the implementation of conditions for peace would be born by the country that bore the main responsibility for warfare. So it became certain in Moscow that Finland would be face to face with the Soviet Union.

The foreign ministers also had an intensive debate on the principle of unconditional surrender. The final outcome of the discussions remained unclear. The foreign ministers of the Western Powers received the impression that Stalin had started to demand unconditional surrender from Finland too.

Stalin was in a strong position when he explained to Roosevelt and Churchill the Soviet demands of Finland during the Teheran summit which began at the end of November 1943. He said that a country which had fought so bravely for her independence had to be taken seriously. He announced that he would demand the 1940 borders, a base at the southernmost tip of Finland and another on the Arctic coast, war reparations, driving out the Germans and the demobilization of the army. The conditions were approximately the same as those that the United States had considered so harsh the previous spring that she did not agree to mediate them to Helsinki.

The Western leaders tried to get a conversation under way on the details for Finland's peace conditions. Roosevelt proposed sugaring the bitter pill by promising Finland Wyborg which was the lively Karelian city demanded by Stalin. Churchill opposed reparations. This subdued discussion indicated to Stalin what he wanted to know: as long as Finland remained independent the West would agree to any conditions whatsoever. It was easy for Stalin to agree to the demand that could be read between the lines. He had had no ideological goals throughout the Continuation

War. The Kuusinen government was already dead and buried during the Winter War.

Stalin expressed this in his own colourful way in Teheran. The Finnish peace negotiator could be Ryti or the devil himself as long as the conditions were met.

TOWARDS
A SOLUTION

The meetings in Moscow and Teheran had decided Finland's fate without the knowledge of the Finns. The Western Allies withdrew from peace negotiations. This promised no good. But they accepted Stalin's idea that Finland was the first exception to the principle of unconditional surrender. This held promise. From the viewpoint of the Allies, too, Finland's war was a separate one for which a political solution was sought. They continued to consider the war against Germany a Crusade with only one solution, a military one.

However, the situation was not simple. Oil and grain are just as important in war as guns and tanks. Finland's foodstuffs and raw material supplies were entirely in German hands. Germany withdrew from the Eastern front but still had strong forces in Northern Finland and in the Baltic States. Finland was in such a tight grip that trying to get free from it would have caused more trouble to Finland than to Germany. Hungary attempted this in April 1944 and fared very badly.

Finland would have to be able to make peace in such a way that it would fulfill the Soviet need for

At the Crossroads

security, would secure Finland's existence and would offer a way out from her relationship with Germany. Finland would have to detach herself from Hitler in such good time that he would not draw Finland into total destruction with him, but at such a late stage that he could not use force against Finland. Finland would have to play a waiting game and then act swiftly.

The military development in Finland's vicinity showed that there was little time left. In January 1944 the Soviet troops broke out of the siege of Leningrad and the Germans began to withdraw from the Baltic states. The Soviet Union recaptured the railway line to Leningrad which meant that she could give proper service to the city and transfer large units of troops to the Karelian Isthmus if she so wished.

Foreign Minister Ramsay summed up Finland's problems in his discussions with the United States' chargé d'affaires: "They are asking me to make the speediest possible peace. They emphasize the word 'speediest', I the word 'possible'". The great question of the year 1944 was whether the opportunity for peace would come sufficiently fast.

Paasikivi Tries

The United States were pulling Finland while the Soviet Union was pushing. Foreign Minister Cordell Hull publicly advised Finland on 8th February 1944 to seek peace negotiations. The Soviet Union began bombing Helsinki. Both countries clearly meant business.

The government sent J.K.Paasikivi to Stockholm to find out what was on offer now. The Soviet Ambassador to Stockholm, Aleksandra

Kollontay mediated Moscow's offer to him. Before negotiations could begin Finland would have to fulfill two conditions; sever her relations with Germany and bring into force their 1940 Peace Treaty. After this details could be negotiated. They included the question of bases in Hanko and Petsamo, demobilization of the army and reparations.

The details were staggering and the situation became even gloomier with the Soviet Union making them public. The prestige of the Kremlin was now also at stake. The government outlined a very careful answer trying to get round the negotiation table in such a way that even the advance conditions could be discussed. This attempt at evasion failed. The Soviet Union responded with a threat; no negotiations before the advance conditions were accepted and Finland had one week to comply with these.

Finland tried tenaciously. The government came up with a skillful response which did not yet approve the advance conditions nor proposed the initiation of negotiations. Finland asked for her representatives to be allowed to hear the Soviet "interpretation" on all conditions including the advance ones. The Kremlin accepted the Finnish request and announced that it would receive two delegates.

It appeared that Finland had gained a tactical evasion victory. Direct contact could be created after all without consenting to harsh terms in advance. However, satisfaction was premature. Paasikivi and a former Foreign Minister, Carl Enckell, were sent to Moscow. They travelled there on 26th March 1944 in the devout belief that the interpretation could alleviate some of the excessive demands. But this was not to be.

Foreign Minister Molotov's discussion with these two old gentlemen was very stern indeed. From Finland's point of view the precise details of all conditions were worse than anticipated. In addition to the demands presented by Kollontay in Stockholm, the Soviet Union gave a very tight schedule for demobilization, valued the reparations at 600 million dollars, gave one month to drive the German troops from Finland, and demanded the cession of Petsamo.

Paasikivi's briefcase was heavy on the way home. After the interpretation the terms were even worse than before it.

<table>
<tr><td>Psychological Bombing</td><td>Finland was in dire straits. Washington publicly pressured for peace and Moscow tightened its terms. But that was not enough. The Soviet Union also increased military pressure which was a direct message to the people of Finland bypassing the government. The strategic air force began bombing Helsinki while Paasikivi was in Stockholm to find out the terms for a possible peace.</td></tr>
</table>

In the three mostly nightly attacks the bombers made more than two thousand flights according to Soviet sources. Helsinki's air defence had just received German radar equipment which was placed on the coast of the Gulf of Finland in such a way that the attacking planes could be observed when they took off from their bases. The air defence had more than eighty guns and about thirty search lights at their disposal. After the first attack the defence included a German night-fighter division based in the Malmi airfield.

The air defence used a method of shooting large barrages in front of the planes before they were above their targets. The intention was to scare the pilots into diverting their planes or into dropping their bombs prematurely. The defence worked excellently. According to Finnish calculations the Soviet planes brought about 16 000 bombs but only 800 of them fell on Helsinki itself. Most of them fell into the sea or to the city's Eastern coastal areas.

The people of Helsinki still talk of the great bombing of the city. Its psychological impact was large, for civilian targets had been left very much at peace until then. However, Helsinki's experiences were almost nothing compared to what German cities were experiencing at the same time and especially towards the end of the war. During these three nights a total of 146 people died and 356 were injured in Helsinki. 109 houses were destroyed, 111 fires broke out and 300 buildings received minor damage.

The military impact of the bombing of Helsinki was fairly poor in relation to its scale. But it fulfilled its task politically and psychologically. It did not break the Finns' willingness to fight, rather on the contrary. But it showed that Finland's position had changed very tangibly. That was precisely what it was intended to do.

Finland Still Waits

Paasikivi demanded in desperate terms that the conditions given in the discussions in Moscow be accepted. Initially Tanner cautiously supported Paasikivi, but changed his mind and fell in behind the majority. During the Easter holidays 1944 it appeared that the Social Democratic grass roots did not accept such harsh conditions – nor did other important circles of opinion.

Mannerheim was mainly pondering what kinds of reasons it would be wisest to present in the rejection. He warned that Finland should not emphasize the difficulty in interning German troops. This could be interpreted in such a way that Finland basically had German leanings. He seems to have thought that the amount of reparations would be a reason that would be politically colourless but believable for turning down the conditions.

Basically there were two reasons for rejecting the peace conditions dictated by Moscow. The first was Germany's strength. Hungary had just tried to detach herself from the war with the result that Germany immediately took over power in Budapest. Finland wanted to avoid this fate by all possible means. The second reason was public opinion, in particular the opinion of Karelians, who had returned to their homes in the wake of the Finnish army. Ordinary people were not able to read the direction of the European war from the news although it was discernible between the lines.

The mere starting of negotiations weakened the political position of Linkomies. The Karelians were shocked that the government even talked of ceding the Karelian Isthmus with the army deep in Eastern Karelia. The domestic political outcome for peace negotiations was that both the Prime Minister and Foreign Minister were suspected of being excessively lenient and even unpatriotic.

In May 1944 the three Great Powers gave Hungary, Romania, Bulgaria and Finland a declaration urging them to cease co-operation with Germany. The Allies promised that the post-war situation for these countries would be the more

April 1944

Territory of Germany and its Allies

Territory conquered by the Soviet Union

Territory conquered by the Western Allies

The results of Paasikivi's negotiations in Moscow had to be weighed against the situation in April 1944 where the Soviet Union had recaptured almost all her old territory. In spring Moscow's terms were rejected but in September the Truce was made almost on the same basis. Meanwhile the Western Allies had landed in France and formed a Western front in Europe, Finland had experienced the shock of major warfare on the Karelian Isthmus and the Soviet Union had advanced to the outskirts of Warsaw.

Previous map on page 73.
Following map on page 106.

advantageous the sooner they detached themselves from the war and the more efficiently they would support the Allied war effort.

The declaration did not directly cancel the principle of unconditional surrender. However, for those who were accustomed to interpreting diplomatic texts its wording indicated that this was precisely what was involved. Thus, apart from the Soviet Union, the Western Powers, too, were pressuring Finland to make peace even under harsh terms. If she should let the situation slip from her grasp the alternative would be even harsher – surrender without conditions.

Hitler Threatens

Hitler was furious over Paasikivi's trip to Moscow and immediately discontinued deliveries of grain. A real storm erupted a couple of weeks later for an unpolitical and even minor reason.

In April 1944 a prominent group of Finnish scientists publicly took exception to German troops occupying Estonia for having transferred some of the scientific collections of Tartu University to Germany. The accusation of cultural vandalism deeply injured Hitler who considered himself an artist and cultural politician as well. He had one of his most famous tantrums. Hitler ordered the immediate discontinuation of arms supplies to Finland, but his civil servants found a loophole in its wording. The vital arms exports for supplying the front could continue after all.

In the course of the spring the Finns pacified Germany so that the export limitations expired in practice in early summer. In his letter to Hitler in May, Mannerheim assured that arms delivered to Finland would under no condition fall into Soviet hands. The newspaper *Svenska Pressen* was shut down as quick as lightning when in June it reported on the invasion of Normandy almost entirely based on Western news sources.

The German reaction to Finland's attempt to make peace was after all milder than expected. The Finns had initiated the peace process, but the result was only a series of partial export bans which were ineffective in practice. Germany's cautious moves indicate that she felt that her position had weakened.

Hitler could perhaps have calculated that Stalin would best take care of the loyalty of Germany's comrade-in-arms by setting excessive demands, at least in Finnish eyes, which he in fact did. For Germany the most important thing was that the Finns in general stayed at the front, whatever they might have thought. After all Finland was not so militarily vital to Germany as Hungary was. The forces engaged in the occupation of Hungary were at the same time in a direction that was vital to Germany's war effort. If she had had to transfer her troops to occupy Finland they would permanently have been absent from Central Europe where the war and Germany's fate would be decided upon.

.

ON THE BRINK
OF THE ABYSS

The Miracle of the Karelian Isthmus

The headquarters in Finland were undergoing a doctrinal dispute on how the troops should be divided between Eastern Karelia and the Karelian Isthmus. At the beginning of June a quarter of the strength of the field army, about 75 000 men, was on the Isthmus. The reports by the front line divisions placed there were calmly confident. On 9th June 1944 hell broke loose.

The crushing force of the attack was a dramatic shock to the Finnish soldiers lulled into the routine of trench warfare. The Finns had to immediately withdraw to the main line of defence which was 20 to 30 kilometres behind the front. Defeats in the early days of the operation were enormous and those who survived the worst in one piece were in a state of shock which prevented sensible action. However, the withdrawal was a success in the sense that the main forces remained fit for combat.

Getting over the initial shock sharpened resistance. The divisions transferred from Eastern Karelia to support the Isthmus began to arrive in the crisis area within a week. The Soviet demand for surrender showed that Finland was really fighting for its existence. The material and psychological factors for a determined defence were once more in existence.

Soviet troops occupied Wyborg with surprising ease on 20th June 1944. After this the goals of the Red Army were Lappeenranta and Imatra, and from there a very effective road and railway network opened up a way for the whole of Southern Finland. The Soviet superiority in numbers always sufficed in breaking through when she tried. However, the Finns were able to limit the penetrations in the front in such a way that the Finnish forces withdrew only 5 to 10 kilometres a week.

Between 25th June and 6th July 1944 the fighting culminated some 20 kilometres North East of Wyborg, at Ihantala in a battle unprecedented in Finnish conditions. The artillery played a decisive role in a successful defence. Fire control methods developed by General V.P. Nenonen made it possible to concentrate massive combined artillery fire against enemy units grouping for an attack and to transfer quickly strikes to new targets. In the most hectic stage of fighting more than 250 guns could shoot at the same target.

Efficient and fast-moving fire could disperse the owerwhelming Soviet tank formations often at their starting positions. The Soviet infantry could be held off although the Finns would have had to temporarily withdraw from their positions. The defensive battles at Tali-Ihantala stabilized the front line. Through extreme effort Finland had gained time and the Soviet Union began to run out of it. Her troops were needed elsewhere for tasks which, from the viewpoint of her overall interests, were more important than a deathblow to Finland.

The soldiers had saved the country. Once again the solution was placed in the hands of politicians.

Political Chaos

As soon as the major battle on the Karelian Isthmus had begun Germany considerably increased her arms deliveries and as compensation demanded political commitment. However, arms deliveries started immediately. Dive bombers and anti-tank weapons arrived from Germany to Finland a week after the big battle began.

The military crisis and political chaos culminated during the last week of June. The Soviet Union occupied Wyborg. In addition to arms Finland requested troops from Germany. Finland was putting out feelers to find out Soviet conditions for peace. The Soviet Union demanded surrender. Germany sent her Foreign Minister to demand an agreement of political alliance. The battle for Tali-Ihantala commenced.

The Social Democrats opposed an agreement with Germany saying that peace would have to be made at some point anyway and an agreement with Hitler would make it more difficult. Upholding the theory of a separate war was the more important the more likely it became that Finland would soon have to make a separate peace. Yet everybody shared Mannerheim's view that the front would not hold if Germany stopped her military support to Finland.

A political agreement with Germany could not be presented to Parliament because it would have rejected it. Ryti, Linkomies and Mannerheim concocted a shrewd solution. Ryti sent a personal letter to Hitler assuring him that the government appointed by Ryti would not make a separate peace. Later this letter was called the Ribbentrop Agreement but legally it was a private document, a letter. By consulting prominent legal experts on the Constitution, Risto Ryti made sure in advance that the agreement was not binding if Finland changed Presidents. He cheated Hitler.

The Germans did not notice the constitutional weakness of the President's commitment. Or alternatively they deduced that nothing more could be squeezed out of the Finns in this situation. They accepted Ryti's letter as political commitment. The assault gun brigade and the infantry division sent by Germany had arrived in Finland and began marching to the front even before Ryti had sent his letter.

Ryti's letter blew the last vestiges of Finnish political unanimity to smithereens. Tanner threatened to resign. The peace opposition in Parliament began to prepare an interpellation to explain why such an important state commitment had not been handled by Parliament. However, in the critical moments of war this political dispute could not be openly publicized. Tanner remained in the government and the interpellation was left in the closets of the peace opposition.

The peace opposition demanded Mannerheim for President and Paasikivi for Prime Minister. The government had been planning a somewhat similar arrangement at the beginning of June. The only question remained when would the time be ripe. The intensity of battles continued to increase north of Wyborg. As long as the Tali-Ihantala battles were raging, all political solutions depended on weapons. The outcome of that combat showed the Soviet Union that a military solution to the Finnish problem would be too expensive and too slow.

The Road to Peace

After the Tali-Ihantala defence victory, the fighting gradually became less intense and the front stabilized. By mid-July the Soviet Union ceased her offensive. She began to withdraw her troops from the Karelian Isthmus and announced that peace could be discussed again providing Finland made the initiative. Thus the demand for surrender lasted only three weeks, the time of the most critical fighting. Once the military situation had stabilized the political rules of the game came into operation.

The configuration of the European War was totally different from what it had been in March, the previous occasion peace had been discussed. The Allied landing force had succeeded in converting their beachhead position in Normandy into a real front. After Paasikivi's trip to Moscow, German troops had withdrawn 300–500 kilometres from the Eastern front. German troops fighting in the Baltic States were about to be encircled. Hitler's victory seemed more and more unlikely.

Germany no longer had the power for serious counter-action if Finland were to go back on Ryti's promise. The German infantry division that took part in the defensive battle of the Gulf of Wyborg left Finland at the end of July. After this the only German unit left in Southern Finland was the assault gun division. It had taken part in the battles on the Karelian Isthmus, but it was not suitable for political warfare.

In the course of the spring, the entire Russian front had had to make a dramatic shift. Finland was rapidly left on the Soviet flank. The main emphasis was now on Poland and Berlin towards which the Allies competed to arrive first. It was more and more important for Stalin to settle matters with Finland which was being left in the rear so that political and military strength would suffice for decisive battles to be fought elsewhere.

Structurally the Continuation War ended in the same situation as the Winter War. The resistance of the Finns just about lasted until other matters became more important to Stalin than Finland. A situation of fluctuating balance emerged on the battlefield. Stalin would have needed some extra time and strength to be able to solve the Finnish question militarily but he lacked this little extra time and that little extra strength he badly needed elsewhere.

After the attack on the Karelian Isthmus came to a standstill Stalin announced that peace could once again be discussed provided the Finns took the initiative and changed governments. The Soviet Union wanted nothing to do with Ryti and Tanner. Ryti resigned to make way for peace and Mannerheim. Through an emergency law Parliament elected Mannerheim President. After complicated negotiations the managing director of the Employers' Confederation, Antti Hackzell became Prime Minister. Before the war he had been an envoy to the Soviet Union and Foreign Minister.

Soon after the change in governments, Field-Marshal Wilhelm Keitel came to Mikkeli to present Mannerheim with a high German decoration in recognition of his defensive battles on the Karelian Isthmus. The decoration's shine did not help. Mannerheim told Keitel that Ryti's promise not to make a separate peace did not concern him.

**The Guns
Stop Speaking**

But Mannerheim delayed the final decision for peace negotiations by three weeks. The Soviet preconditions for Truce negotiations meant a breaking off of relations with Germany and disarming its troops. Mannerheim gathered together a group of negotiators which included more war-time top decision makers than the foreign policy leadership of the new government. The atmosphere was gloomy but they decided to accept the preconditions.

The country was led by old men who were forced to the extreme limits of their mental and physical endurance. Hackzell had to announce over the radio that Finland had broken off her relations with Germany in accordance with Soviet demands. He mixed up the sheets of his manuscript in such a way that this, diplomatically its most important content, remained unread although it was included in the speech he gave to Parliament the same morning. To crown it all, the new Foreign Minister Carl Enckell forgot to mediate the official information to the Soviet Union that a decision to break off relations had been taken and that this decision had been announced to Parliament.

On 3rd September 1944, late in the evening, Finland's envoy to Stockholm, G.A.Gripenberg, the Cabinet Secretary of the Swedish Foreign Ministry, Erik Boheman and a Soviet Legation Counsellor, Vladimir Semyonov, together drew up an official announcement that Finland had broken off relations with Germany. The Soviet Union committed herself to ceasing hostilities the following morning at eight provided that Finland gave notification of its intentions at once. The phrasing of the declaration was rapidly conveyed to the press and radio in Helsinki. At the same

time the troops at the front were ordered to cease
fire on 4th September 1944 at eight a.m. and this
was carried out. Moscow did not receive in time
the message that this notification had been publicized and continued firing on the front 24 hours
after the Finns had ceased fire.

It was in the morning of 5th September 1944
that silence prevailed on the fronts. But it was not
peace yet.

THE BEGINNING
OF A NEW ROAD

The Truce of Moscow

In accordance with the principle agreed upon at the Teheran Summit Meeting, the Soviet Union presented her allies with the truce conditions she had set for Finland. The United States took no stand but there was a long discussion about them between London and Moscow. The Soviet Union would have wanted to make a peace treaty proper whereas Britain wanted only a truce. The compromise was a truce and an agreement that the conditions of the Truce would be made more specific. The protocol problem that arose from signing this Truce was solved in such a way that Britain authorised the Soviet Colonel-General N.A. Zhdanov to sign it on behalf of the British Empire.

With Britain and the Soviet Union solving their common problems, Finland's peace delegation had to idly wait in Moscow. The pressure exceeded Prime Minister Hackzell's endurance. He suffered an apoplectic fit from which he did not recover.

The Kremlin's main negotiator was Foreign Minister Molotov and he took an extremely strict line. The Finns were like schoolboys caught up to no good in front of a very angry headmaster. Before the actual dictation of conditions there was a nerve-wracking dispute over the position of German troops in Finland. Molotov harassed the Finns mercilessly with detailed information which in his view indicated that the promise of breaking off relations with Germany were unfulfilled. Due to poor communications the Finns could not properly respond to Molotov's very consistent accusations.

The situation was unbearable for the Finns but the Germans solved the problem without knowing it. They tried to occupy Suursaari in the middle of the Gulf of Finland. The Finns fought off the landing in a fierce battle. This was Finland's only trump in the Moscow negotiations. The battle showed that the Finns really intended to change course and also to oppose Germany militarily.

The actual negotiations were very simple. The Finns' counterarguments and attempts to make the outlines presented by the Soviet Union more precise generally led nowhere. The Finns were only able to prolong the period of paying war reparations from five to six years and to acquire two extra weeks for demobilization.

The negotiations ended with the familiar threatening demand. There was so little time for signing the agreement that the names of the negotiators were already on paper before proper authority granted by Parliament had arrived.

The agreement was harsher than the proposal rejected in the spring. It returned the Eastern border to the post–Winter War line but in addition Finland lost Petsamo and the Soviet Navy Base was transferred from Hanko to Porkkala, a few dozen kilometres from Helsinki. The

97

sum total of reparations that had shocked Finns in the spring had been dropped to a half or at least that is how it was recorded on paper.

In addition to orders to cease hostilities, orders concerning new borders and reparations, the Truce also regulated many such things that ordinarily are included in a final peace settlement and not always even in that. According to this Finland agreed:

– to hand over airfields and harbours
– to demobilize the field army in two and a half months
– to sentence war criminals
– to release political prisoners
– to disband "fascist-like" organizations
– to abolish regulations limiting political activities
– to compensate for the property transferred from the ceded area
– to hand over German property in Finland
– to pay the expenses of the Control Commission.

Even if the document was harsher than the one that emerged in the previous negotiations it was indefinitely milder than the demand for surrender presented in June. This was the most central content of the Truce. It was not a document for surrender but an agreement.

The War in Lapland

The Germans withdrew from southern Finland voluntarily on the date set as the time limit in the preconditions of the Truce, 15th December 1944. Their troops were north of the Oulu-Kajaani line, but that area they dominated in practice. The Truce ordered that the Finns would have to drive them away from there too or disarm them. It was a Truce which contained the responsibility of starting a new war.

Molotov's accusations of fraternizing with the Germans were well founded. The liaison officer sent by the General Headquarters to Rovaniemi after negotiations with the Germans agreed a schedule according to which they would withdraw. The Finnish troops followed peacefully at a suitable distance. This make-belief war called the autumn manoeuvre could be continued until the Control Commission arrived in Helsinki. Then it became a question in earnest. The Soviet Union simultaneously demanded efficient warfare and demobilization.

In his dual role of President and Commander-in-Chief, Mannerheim was between the devil and the deep blue sea. The commander of the Finnish forces in Lapland, Lieutenant General Hjalmar Siilasvuo decided to start fighting with a surprise landing at Tornio behind the German lines. The attempt was militarily foolhardy and so dangerous that the duty of a responsible Commander-in-Chief would have been to forbid it. On the other hand the President had to comply with the Commission's demand for efficient warfare and the landing of Siilasvuo's troops was precisely that.

Mannerheim left the Colonel who was Head of the Operations Department at the Headquarters and the General leading the war in Lapland to solve the dispute among themselves. He knew that the General would beat the Colonel. The landing succeeded and the Finns held the initiative in Lapland momentarily. It was a vital political war manoeuvre but militarily the war in Lapland was an agonizing toil.

The Germans had more than 200 000 men, 25 000 motor vehicles and 30 000 horses in

Lapland. And they had a carefully prepared plan for withdrawal. What the Finns called the war in Lapland meant just the implementation of that plan for the Germans.

The Finns normally got stuck in front of the defensive positions constructed by the Germans in very narrow stretches of road. The Finns had no other option than to outflank them. While the Finns were trudging along bogs and marshes the Germans detached themselves from their positions, blew up bridges, laid mines on the roads, and drove off. The Finns pursued them on bicycles with no equipment until they came up against another defensive position and had to outflank them once more.

The Germans considered the landing at Tornio a vile betrayal and in revenge began to destroy Lapland. Initially the order only concerned state buildings but later all houses.

The Finns were not essentially able to speed up the German withdrawal but did cause the loss of about four thousand men of whom less than a thousand fell. The Germans withdrew to Norway in the Utsjoki region towards the end of November 1944, but only in April 1945 from the Kilpisjärvi region.

The Control Commission

The Allied Control Commission dominated the political and psychological everyday life of the Finns at least as strongly as the government did. Its task was to monitor Finland's compliance with the regulations of the Truce. In accordance with the internal division of labour of the Allies, the Soviet Union exercised the Commission's authority. Britain sent three youngish officers as her representative. Their task was mainly symbolic and their position very awkward. The Soviets kept them completely in the sidelines. They obtained their information even on important matters from the Finnish authorities or from newspapers.

The Commission's status was peculiar. It had the right to examine the actions of all Finnish authorities but lacked direct power. Thus it could only mediate its observations and demands to the Finnish government. In principle it was the staff of an occupying army without troops. In practice it had the highest political power in Finland but the country was governed in accordance with the rules and regulations of a Western Democracy and Nordic Parliamentarism.

The Chairman of the Control Commission was Andrei Zhdanov, the Colonel General who had signed the Truce on behalf of not only the Soviet Union but also of Great Britain. His status in the Kremlin was very strong. He was even considered a possible successor to Stalin. In summer 1940 Zhdanov led the Sovietization of Estonia. This was an experience the Finns did not appreciate. Sending such a central figure to Finland was considered a bad omen. On the other hand a politically strong chairman was beneficial to Finland. He was able to make decisions when negotiating. And if he got the impression that Finland had her cards on the table his word carried real weight in the Kremlin.

The Commission's overall strength was less than 200 officers and officials of whom more than 150 were Soviets. In accordance with the Truce Finland had to pay for its offices and transportation.

Naturally the Commission was psychologically and politically much heavier a burden than economically. Yet it was not nearly such a millstone as the entire occupying armies that the other countries on the losing side had to bear.

The Government Takes a Grip

One of the reasons for turning down the peace conditions in spring 1944 was that the reparations of 600 million dollars seemed impossible. In the September agreement the sum had dropped by half although the other conditions became harder. Later in the course of the autumn it appeared that the Soviets meant the 1938 gold dollar and calculated the value of deliveries at the pre-war price level. In practice this meant that the real value of reparations was about 600 million dollars anyway.

The question of reparations was the worst stumbling block for Castrén's government. Castrén's administrative law and Zhdanov's military inflexibility were at loggerheads and the negotiations became badly bogged down. Things started to look up when Mannerheim agreed to appoint a new government with J.K.Paasikivi as Prime Minister.

After the change in government the Commission's attitude changed, and this showed the important basic factor of post-war politics. The Commission was flexible if it could trust the Finns. It did not bend under pressure. Soon after the appointment of Paasikivi's government, the Commission agreed to review the pricing of reparations and to reduce them by 10 – 15 per cent to Finland's advantage. The agreement on this basis was enormously heavy but the emergence of an agreement in general was a significant political relief.

Demobilization of the field army was another big problem of autumn 1944. The Finns tried over and over again to explain to the Commission how illogical it was to demand both efficient war in Lapland and demobilization at the same time. The Soviet response was simple. Conduct the war in Lapland so efficiently that both the war and demobilization can be concluded within the set time limit.

At the planning stage of demobilization another problem arose concerning the pre-war strength of the army indicated in the Truce. The Finns interpreted it to mean the strength in spring 1941 before the Continuation War, i.e. nearly 64 000 men. The Soviets adhered to their interpretation of the wording that the strength meant the situation that had prevailed before the Winter War, i.e half of the number preceding the Continuation War.

The Commission's interpretation won. But the dispute took time. When the solution emerged there was only one and a half months left for demobilization. The Finns undertook this desperate task determinedly and systematically, succeeding in sticking to the time table that had seemed impossible. On 5th December 1944 they announced in dry military terms that the mission was accomplished. It appears that this achievement made an impression on the Commission officers both professionally and politically.

About the time the army was being demobilized the Soviet Union publicly showed her satisfaction with Finnish actions for the first time. When Paasikivi's government had got a proper grip on affairs it began to be seen that the Commission's political attitude was not quite what Finns had feared.

The Commission's political advisor Pavel Orlov assured an American journalist in October that the Soviet aim was not Sovietization: "... we want an independent but friendly Finland", he said and also explained why: "since 1940 the Soviet Union has learnt a lot". Naturally it was politically advantageous for the Soviet Union to present this kind of facade to the West. But in practice too it functioned in accordance with Orlov's words.

The Stronghold of Peace and Democracy

In autumn 1944 the Communists established the left wing's joint election organization, SKDL. Its aim was to secure Communist leadership in the left wing movement and in the entire new politics.

Behind this official facade the basic question was whether the same kind of united front of Communists and non-communists would emerge in Finland as in many Eastern European countries where broadly-based configurations of Peoples' Fronts gradually drifted under the leadership of the Communists and directed development to a Peoples' Democracy. The basic idea of the Communist-led SKDL was to secure precisely this kind of development. However, the plan collapsed immediately for the Social Democratic SDP refused an election alliance with SKDL. From the very beginning Finland's road differed from that of Czechoslovakia. In Finland the Communists' main opponent was another workers' party.

The SDP had something with which the Communists could not compete. It did not live from the mere ideology of socialism. It could appeal to national unity and comradeship of arms experienced during the war. Therefore its message was listened to by others than workers alone. Because of its common national background its message felt credible also in the ears of those who did not vote for it.

The life of war-weary Finns was in many ways bleak, yet the country was a stronghold of peace and democracy on the northern periphery of a Europe ravaged by dictatorships and war. As the Finns prepared themselves for the elections of March 1945, the Western Allied forces were still fighting on the Rhine and the Soviet troops in the Eastern part of Germany. Dresden experienced heavy bombing in which probably more people died than in the first nuclear attack on Hiroshima in August. The V 2-missiles developed by Germany were still being used. The last missiles from continental Europe to the British Isles were launched after Finland's elections.

Much more than the relative power of Finnish parties was measured in these elections. The West wanted to see whether a country that had just waged war alongside Hitler could really get its democracy to function. For her part, the Soviet Union wanted to see the real political compass reading in these elections; whether the country was ready for such a profound change of course as its new leaders proclaimed. What was involved for the Finns themselves was whether the country could continue on the basis of Scandinavian Democracy.

On all these scales of measurement Finland fared laudably. The elections were conducted in an exemplary manner according to all the rules of democracy. The West obtained proof measured in figures that Finland was a different matter

March 1945

■ Territory of Germany and
its Allies

▤ Territory conquered by
the Soviet Union

▥ Territory conquered by
the Western Allies

The Parliamentary elections held in March 1945 in
Finland were a peaceful exception in a Europe waging
war. Germany had been forced back nearly to her old
territory and the major part of Italy was held by the
Allies. But there was fighting in both areas. Finnish
democracy gained a lead over the losers but also over
the winners of the war.

Previous map on page 85.

from the Eastern European countries that had fallen within the Soviet sphere of influence. The Soviet Union saw from the election results that a political change of course really had taken place. And, to the relief of the majority, the Finns noted that Parliament remained in the hands of the old basic parties. A parliamentarily strong coalition of the three biggest parties emerged which Paasikivi continued to lead. One of these coalition parties in the government were the Communists. Its two equally large partners were the Social Democrats and the Agrarian League both of which supported Nordic Parliamentarism and Western democracy.

However, the internal tension did not disappear in the spring elections of 1945, but it was channeled through proper Parliamentary procedures.

A total of 90 000 Finns died or were lost in the Winter and Continuation Wars and 3 900 were left prisoners of war. The share of those fallen in the wars of the then population of Finland was slightly below 2.5 per cent. It is clearly less than in the Central European countries that took part in the war. For example in Poland and Germany this ratio was over ten per cent, whereas in Czechoslovakia and Holland it was about the same level as in Finland.

Finland's civilian population got off clearly lighter than other European countries'. Only less than 3 000 of them died which is less than 3 per cent of all victims of the war. In the European areas ravaged worst by war, more civilians were killed than soldiers. The collective memory of the Finns still recalls the major bombings on Helsinki

The Price of War

in February 1944, however, 146 people were killed in them. In two nights in Dresden apparently 100 000 Germans were killed.

The losses made mortality rates higher than birth rates in the three phases of the war; during the Winter War of 1939–40, in the offensive period of the Continuation War in late summer and autumn 1941, and during the major battles on the Karelian Isthmus in early summer 1944. The war losses changed the demography of the country predominantly female which has had broad social and demographic consequences right up until the present time.

A total of less than 190 000 were wounded in the wars. About 50 000 of them remained invalids for the rest of their lives. It is estimated that 20 000 of these men will still be alive by the year 2000. Then the average age of war invalids will be more than eighty years.

Reparations

The interpretation that the Soviet Union gave in the autumn 1944 on the pricing basis of reparations raised their real value in excess of more than 15 per cent compared with the figure that Finns had understood was their commitment under the Truce. Later the Soviet Union alleviated the pricing, extended the payment period and lowered the sums of reparations in such a way that by autumn 1952 the real value of deliveries to the Soviet Union was about 25 per cent below the value determined in the Truce.

The engineering industry had to bear the greatest brunt of reparations. Machines and ships accounted for about 60 per cent of the total value. Finland's traditional industry, forestry, accounted for only 27 per cent. Although war reparations were a real burden and speeded up the structural change in Finnish industry, they nevertheless freed the main bulk of wood processing industry production for exports to the West which was necessary to secure the supply of raw materials for the reparations industry and the whole country.

The economic burden of the war reparations were at their heaviest in 1945 when they made up between 6–7 per cent of the GNP. After 1948 their share was less than 4 per cent and in the early 1950s it was only about 2 per cent. These shares do not seem high but they compelled the whole economy to work continuously and at a forced tempo.

The Refugee Question

Finland lost 12 per cent of her land area under the Truce. All the 400 000 people from the territory ceded to the Soviet Union moved to what remained of Finland, to look for a new place to live and work. More than half of them had worked in agriculture.

The government launched the preparations for a new land acquisition law at express speed and the old Parliament ratified it in spring 1945 on its last day in office. It stipulated that 10 per cent of smaller farms could be expropriated for resettlement and in the biggest farms it could be as much as 75 per cent. The evacuees had the priority for land acquisition but it could also be handed over to soldiers returning from the front as well as war widows and orphans.

The Act on Land Acquisition implemented a land reform in Finland which is among the most profound in Europe. The task of resettling evacuees was a greater burden on the economy than the reparations and it was carried out at a surprising speed. By 1947, well over half of the evacuees had obtained a new homestead and by the end of 1948, 95 per cent. At that time there were four years left to pay war reparations. Finland was a shining example in the dismal history of refugee questions. She was able to solve them without political upheaval. She tried something which nobody had dared to try before and was almost surprised herself that it was nearly a complete success.

A successful resettlement policy was a significant achievement in foreign politics. The ceded province stopped being Finnish when Finns moved away. The government's bold and prompt moves to relocate the refugees in their new homesteads showed to the Soviet Union that Karelia is not irredenta to Finland.

The Balance Sheet of War

The faultlessly conducted elections in spring 1945 and a government that brightly reflected their result showed an exceptional political stability and functioning democracy in a post-war Europe. The emergence of a government of the big three parties was a turning point indicating that the Finnish Constitution and political institutions were still able to function despite the war and political pressure. Many countries that fought on the winning side were not able to maintain such political continuity as did Finland.

For a long time after the war it was customary to say in Finland that the country's problems originated from two lost wars. Indeed this saying describes the political situations in which Finland found herself after the Winter and Continuation Wars. But militarily she did not lose either war although she was forced into a tight position. In both situations she secured her main political goal, independence. Finland was never occupied during the wars. In a Europe devastated by the Second World War there were three countries involved whose capitals never experienced foreign tanks rumbling on their streets: Moscow, London and Helsinki.

Throughout the war period Finland was badly undermanned in her relative strength but she compensated for the lack of power with determined and unscrupulously bold diplomacy. She could militarily delay the Soviet Union always to the extent that other things became more important to the Kremlin than Finland. And in some situations forces beyond her control came to her aid.

Three things are needed in a war: military power in sufficient relationship to the circumstances, political intelligence which does not fear even the worst conditions and good luck. Finland had all of them. During a major war the basis for security policy is the same as in peace time although the methods for conducting politics are exceptional. States assess their interests in a coldly rational manner and act accordingly. Big states can do this by moulding the political conditions of a whole continent and even of the whole world. Small states have to adapt to the prevailing conditions, but adapting is not the same as submission.